Frommer's®

P9-ELV-619

100

Places to Take Your Kids
Before They Grow Up

4th Edition

by Holly Hughes & Julie Duchaine

WILEY

John Wiley & Sons, Inc.

Contents

Published by:

John Wiley & Sons, Inc.

111 River St.
Hoboken, NJ 07030-5774

ISBN 978-1-118-16492-1

Editor: Leslie A. Shen with Andrea Kahn
Production Editor: Michael Brumitt
Photo Editors: Alden Gewirtz and John Vorwald
Cover Photo Editor: Richard Fox
Interior book design: Melissa Auciello-Brogan
Production by Wiley Indianapolis Composition Services

Front cover photo: Boy jumping in Arches National Park. ©Ann Cutting / Workbook Stock / Getty Images
Back cover photo: Mother, son, and dog walking by Beartooth Lake in the Rocky Mountains of Wyoming. ©Gordon Wiltsie / National Geographic / Getty Images

For information on our other products and services or to obtain technical support, please contact our Customer Care Department within the U.S. at 877/762-2974; outside the U.S. at 317/572-3993 or fax 317/572-4002.

Wiley also publishes its books in a variety of electronic formats. Some content that appears in print may not be available in electronic formats.

Manufactured in the United States of America

5 4 3 2 1

About the Author

Holly Hughes has traveled the globe as an editor and writer. A former executive editor of Fodor's Travel Publications, she edits the annual *Best Food Writing* anthology and is the author of the bestselling *Frommer's 500 Places to Take Your Kids Before They Grow Up*, *Frommer's 500 Places to See Before They Disappear*, and *Frommer's New York City with Kids*. She has also written fiction for middle graders. New York City makes a convenient jumping-off place for her travels with her three children and husband.

About the Co-Author

Julie Duchaine has been a freelance writer for the past 25 years. Most recently, she contributed to *Frommer's 500 Places to See Before They Disappear* and *Frommer's 500 Places for Food & Wine Lovers*. She lives in Milwaukee.

Acknowledgments

Many thanks to all my fellow parents whose brains I picked for travel suggestions over the past 4 years. You were so generous with your trip memories, I almost felt in some cases as if I had traveled there with you. And to all the other parents who had to listen to my enthusiastic ramblings by the coffee urns at PTA meetings and on the soccer field sidelines—thank you for never letting your eyes glaze over as I raved on and on about yet another far-flung destination you really should visit.

I've also relied on the devoted corps of Frommer's writers to supply me with phone numbers, addresses, and recommendations of their own favorite family destinations. Your descriptions have been invaluable—you're the real experts in your various parts of the world, and I'm beholden to you.

And finally, I have to thank my husband and children, who not only put up with Mom disappearing into her office for hours at a time but are also the best travel companions I could ever ask for.

—Holly Hughes

I would like to thank my co-writer, Holly Hughes for sharing her knowledge and providing helpful suggestions over the course of many long phone calls.

I also owe a debt to my editors, who kept everything on track and running smoothly.

Finally, I would like to thank the Frommer's writers whose work was invaluable when it came time to supply phone numbers and hotel suggestions. Their work made mine easier, and I am grateful for that.

—Julie Duchaine

An Invitation to the Reader

In researching this book, we discovered many wonderful places. We're sure you'll find others. Please tell us about them, so we can share the information with your fellow travelers in upcoming editions. If you were disappointed with a recommendation, we'd love to know that, too. Please write to:

Frommer's 100 Places to Take Your Kids Before They Grow Up, 4th Edition
John Wiley & Sons, Inc. • 111 River St. • Hoboken, NJ 07030-5774
frommersfeedback@wiley.com

Advisory & Disclaimer

Frommer's Icons

We use four feature icons to help you quickly find the information you're looking for. At the end of each review, look for:

 Where to get more information

✈ Nearest airport

🚄 Nearest train station

🛏 Recommended kid-friendly hotels

Travel Resources at Frommers.com

Frommer's travel resources don't end with this guide. Frommer's website, **www.frommers.com**, has travel information on more than 4,000 destinations. We update features regularly, giving you access to the most current trip-planning information and the best airfare, lodging, and car-rental bargains. You can also listen to podcasts, connect with other Frommers.com members through our active-reader forums, share your travel photos, read blogs from guidebook editors and fellow travelers, and much more.

About This Book

Why These 100 Places?

The obvious question just about everybody asked me when I told them I was writing this book: "Have you been to all 100 places?" I regret to say I haven't—not yet—but I've been to a surprising number of them over the past few years. If not, I've talked to other families who have generously shared their travel memories with me. Immersed in writing this book, at times I almost imagined we had been everyplace. But I have to say, now that it's written, I'm glad we haven't seen it all and done it all yet—we still have a few traveling years ahead of us as a family, and now we've got a thicker file than ever of thrilling trips to look forward to.

Of course, choosing a destination is only part of the challenge. Knowing what it's like to travel with youngsters, I've tried to give you the tools you need to make these trips unforgettable. I've dug up tidbits of history or other background, so you can look like experts when you're leading your children around a site. It's not enough just to go to a place—you've got to imagine how the people of this distant era lived, why one army won this battle and not the other, what makes this park different from that one, which animals thrive where. You do it to keep the kids interested, and then somehow you find yourself having a richer experience of the place, too. Awakening that sense of wonder is what travel is all about, for adults as well as children.

I've also suggested strategies for certain destinations—whether or not to hire a tour guide (some enrich the experience, others bog you down in boring details); whether to drive, walk, or take the tram; whether to dawdle over a museum's every exhibit or zero in on a few key displays. With the proper strategy, you'd be surprised how much even young children can delight in these destinations. Don't sell them short! The payoff is all cumulative—the more your children travel, the more they'll observe and appreciate on further trips, and the more intriguing trips you'll be able to plan.

Of course, you are the experts when it comes to knowing your own family's interests—whether they be history, culture, nature, or outdoor adventure—so rather than follow a geographic scheme, I've organized this book in groups of destinations with a similar emphasis, spread around the globe. After a successful trip to one destination, I hope you'll consider planning new trips to others in that category—chances are you'll like them too.

The geographic index in the back will help you match nearby destinations, so you can take in a whole cluster of sights on one vacation.

Hotels

I wish I'd had space to give you full-blown hotel reviews, but you can rely on these choices being the most family-friendly lodgings in the area. Traveling with a family is not cheap, so I tend to recommend moderately priced hotels rather than the most expensive lodgings. (You don't need my help in finding the poshest hotel in town—what's hard to find is the small hotel with no advertising budget.) I also recommend modern, plainly furnished hotels rather than antique-laden B&Bs, which, for all their charm, may not welcome children. The other criteria I look for: kitchenettes, room service, room layouts that accommodate extra beds, TVs in the room, and the trump card, a swimming pool (give us a good pool and my kids will accept almost anything). Price ranges of course are relative. The three price ranges I note— $$$ (expensive), $$ (moderate), and $ (inexpensive)—don't conform to one set of dollar equivalents, but rather reflect the local market. A $125-per-night motel room in South Dakota would seem expensive, but if you can find something clean and safe at that price in New York City, snap it up. For fuller descriptions (and other useful travel info), please consult the corresponding Frommer's guides for these destinations.

Age Ranges

For each destination, I've also indicated an age range for children. When I say "All ages," that means you could bring a baby or young toddler in a stroller and not feel out of place. I'm not saying the 6-month-old would get much out of the experience (!), but at least you could take older siblings there without the baby being a hindrance. In a few cases, I've upped the age range on a destination if it somehow poses challenges handled best by older kids. I admit that these recommended age ranges are subjective—for lack of a more objective test, I've based them on what my own children would have been interested in at what age. My kids have become good travelers over the years. Yours can be too.

They're only young once, so see the world through their eyes—you won't regret it!

The Grand Canyon
Where the Earth Splits Open
All Ages • Arizona

POSTCARDS JUST DON'T DO JUSTICE TO THIS CLASSIC AMERICAN PANorama—this majestic 277-mile-long canyon of the Colorado River, an enormous primeval gash in the earth's crust. Gaze down into its depth from the rim and you'll see striated bands of multicolored rock, a living history of geologic periods unfolding at your feet. Descend into it and you'll pass through no less than four distinct climate zones, as if you began your day in Mexico and ended it in Alaska.

The Grand Canyon attracts a staggering number of tourists every year, many of whom simply view the panorama from the North or South Rim viewpoints and then drive on. While it's awesome indeed to gaze around from the rim, something about that monumental chasm makes me long to climb down in. There are any number of hiking trails, from 7 to 9 miles long; if taking on the river is more your style, check the park website for a list of approved commercial outfitters that run 3- to 18-day rafting trips, from placid floats to heart-stopping whitewater thrill rides.

Perhaps the most memorable way to explore the Grand Canyon is to pick your way down the steep, narrow trails on the back of an ornery mule. The best options for kids depart from the North Rim and are offered by **Canyon Trail Rides** (✆ 435/679-8665; www.canyonrides.com). These rides range from 1-hour scenic rides along the rim to half-day trips (either a longer rim route or one that heads 2,300 ft. down the North Kaibab Trail). The real classics, though, are 1- or 2-night packages that go to the bottom of the canyon and include sleeping arrangements and simple meals at **Phantom Ranch,** the only lodging available below the rim of the Grand Canyon. These Phantom Ranch trips fill up soon after reservations are accepted, 13 months in advance (call ✆ **888/297-2757** or visit www.grandcanyonlodges.com). For possible openings the next day, call the **Bright Angel Transportation Desk** at © **928/ 638-2631,** ext. 6015. Riders must be at least 4 feet 7 inches tall and under 200 pounds; pregnant women are not allowed.

A fair number of visitors also buzz overhead in sightseeing planes and helicopters. **Grand Canyon Airlines** (© **866/235- 9422** or 928/638-2359; www.grandcanyonairlines.com) is the granddaddy of scenic air tours out here. **Papillon Grand Canyon** (© **888/635-7272** or 928/638-2419; www.papillon.com) operates planes and helicopters, both from the rim of the canyon and from Las Vegas. The truly heart-stopping moment is when you're look- ing down at the treetops of the Kaibab National Forest, and then you cross the North Rim of the canyon and—whoosh!—the ground drops away suddenly beneath you, an effect more spectacular in person than any IMAX film could ever convey.

ⓘ © **928/638-7888;** www.nps.gov/grca.

✈ Grand Canyon National Park, Tusayan. Flagstaff Pulliam, 85 miles. Phoenix Sky Harbor International, 228 miles.

🛏 $$$ **El Tovar Hotel,** South Rim (© **888/297-2757** or 928/ 638-2631; www.grandcanyonlodges.com). $$ **Grand Canyon Lodge,** North Rim (© **877/386-4383** or 928/638-2611; www. grandcanyonforever.com).

WHY THEY'LL THANK YOU: Discovering what's in that hole in the ground.

Postcard Panoramas

2

The Redwood Forests of California

All ages • Crescent City, California

IT'S HARD TO EXPLAIN THE FEELING YOU GET IN THE OLD-GROWTH forests of **Redwood National and State Parks.** Everything seems big, misty, and primeval—flowering bushes cover the ground, 10-foot-tall ferns line the creeks, and the smells are rich and musty. It's so Jurassic Park, you half expect to turn the corner and see a dinosaur.

The scientific name for these massive conifers is Sequoia sempervirens, cousins of the giant sequoias (see Sequoia National Park, **3**). Sheathed in rough reddish bark, miraculously fire-resistant, their stout straight trunks shoot up 100 feet or more before a canopy of branches begins; they often reach a total height of more than 300 feet. Among the planet's most ancient individuals—the oldest dated coast redwood is more than 2,200 years old—they only grow in temperate rainforests, meaning nowhere but the U.S. Pacific Coast. In 1968, the federal government created Redwood National Park (nowadays combined with three state redwood parks) to protect what's left of this seriously endangered species. The relative isolation of this stretch of coast helped the forests survive intact, but it also makes for a long drive.

The most spectacular display is along the **Avenue of the Giants,** a 31-mile stretch of U.S. 101 through the **Humboldt Redwoods State Park** (© **707/946-2263;** www.humboldtredwoods.org). Environmentalists bemoan the tacky attractions along this route, but youngsters love 'em—from south to north, hollow **Chimney Tree,** where J.R.R. Tolkien's Hobbit is rumored to live; **One-Log House,** a small dwelling built inside a log; and the **Shrine Drive-Thru Tree.** More dignified landmarks include **Founders Grove,** honoring those who started the Save the Redwoods League in 1918; and the 950-year-old **Immortal Tree.** Don't settle for looking at all this out your car window—from many parking areas you can ramble on short loop trails into awesome redwood groves.

The other cluster of parks begins another 100 miles or so farther north, threaded along U.S. Hwy. 101. The most scenic drive parallels 101, along the **Newton B. Drury Scenic Parkway,** passing through redwood groves and meadows where Roosevelt elk graze, and **Coastal Drive,** which has grand views of the Pacific. But again, the truly spine-tingling experience requires getting out and hiking through these soaring perpendicular woods. Pick up a park map to find your way to **Tall Trees Trail,** a 3¼-mile round-trip to a 600-year-old tree often touted as the world's tallest (get a permit at the Redwood Information Center in Orick); the self-guided mile-long **Lady Bird Johnson Grove Loop;** the short, very popular

Wandering among the giants of Redwood National Park.

Fern Canyon Trail; or, for the littlest hikers, the .25-mile-long **Big Tree Trail,** a paved trail leading to—what else?—a big tree.

ⓘ 1111 Second St. (𝓬 **707/464-6101;** www.nps.gov/redw).

✈ Del Norte County Regional, Crescent City.

🛏 $ **Curly Redwood Lodge,** 701 Redwood Hwy. S. (U.S. 101), Crescent City (𝓬 **707/464-2137;** www.curlyredwoodlodge.com). $$$ **Lost Whale Inn,** 3452 Patrick's Point Dr., Trinidad (𝓬 **800/ 677-7859** or 707/677-3425; www.lostwhaleinn.com).

WHY THEY'LL THANK YOU: Seeing the redwoods before they're gone.

Postcard Panoramas

3

Sequoia & Kings Canyon National Parks
Giant Trees of the Sierras
All ages • Visalia & Fresno, California

Oɴʟʏ 200 ᴍɪʟᴇs ʙʏ ʀᴏᴀᴅ ꜰʀᴏᴍ ᴏꜰᴛᴇɴ-ᴏᴠᴇʀʀᴜɴ Yᴏsᴇᴍɪᴛᴇ Nᴀᴛɪᴏɴᴀʟ Park, **Sequoia** and **Kings Canyon** national parks still feel like untrammeled wilderness. Only one road, the Generals Highway, loops through the area, and no road traverses the Sierra here. High-altitude hiking and backpacking are what these parks are really all about; some 700 miles of trails traverse this terrain of snowcapped Sierra Nevada peaks (including Mount Whitney, which at 14,494 ft. is the highest point in the lower 48 states), high-country lakes, and alpine meadows. For families, though, there's one main attraction: the largest groves of giant sequoias in the Sierra Nevada.

Though they are two separate parks, Sequoia and Kings Canyon are contiguous and managed jointly from the park headquarters at Ash Mountain—you hardly know when you're leaving one and entering the other.

Of the 75 or so groves of giant sequoias in the parks, the two most convenient to visit are **Grant Grove** (in Kings Canyon, near the Big Stump park entrance), and **Giant Forest** (in Sequoia, 16 miles from the Ash Mountain entrance). In Grant Grove, a 100-foot walk through the hollow trunk of the **Fallen Monarch** makes a fascinating side trip. The tree has been used for shelter for more than 100 years and is tall enough inside that you can walk through without bending over. In Giant Forest, the awesome **General Sherman Tree** is considered the largest living thing in the world; single branches of this monster are more than 7

Kings Canyon National Park.

feet thick. Giant Forest has some 40 miles of intersecting footpaths to wander; the 6-mile **Trail of the Sequoias** will take you to the grove's far eastern end, where you'll find some of the finest trees.

While Sequoia's primary attraction is those incredible trees, Kings Canyon Park encompasses the **deepest canyon in the United States:** Drive to Road's End on the Kings Canyon Highway (open late April to early Nov) to stand by the banks of the Kings River and stare up at granite walls rising thousands of feet above the river.

ⓘ Ash Mountain entrance, CA 198 from Visalia. Big Stump entrance, CA 180 from Fresno (② **559/565-3341;** www.nps.gov/seki or www.sequoia-kingscanyon.com).

✈ Fresno Yosemite International, 53 miles.

🛏 $ **Dorst Campground,** in Sequoia, near Giant Forest (② **877/444-6777**). $$ **Wuksachi Village & Lodge,** 64740 Wuksachi Way, Sequoia National Park (② **866/807-3598** or 801/559-4948 [international]; www.visitsequoia.com).

WHY THEY'LL THANK YOU: The redwoods' awesome (and even more endangered) cousins.

Devils Tower
Something Strange in Wyoming
All ages • Devils Tower, Wyoming

I KNEW MY KIDS WOULD LOVE THE SCENE IN *CLOSE ENCOUNTERS OF THE Third Kind* when Richard Dreyfuss starts sculpting Devils Tower out of mashed potatoes. Spielberg sure picked the right natural landing pad for his alien spaceship to make contact with earthlings—there is something otherworldly about this stark monolith rising out of the Wyoming pines and prairies. The Northern Plains Indians called it Bears Lodge, and it has sacred meanings for them too. Even seeing a picture of it is unforgettable, but visiting **Devils Tower** in person—well, that's more special than you'd imagine.

Time for a geology lesson. Devils Tower is what's known as an igneous intrusion, meaning that it's a column of rock hardened by molten lava that seeped long ago into a vein of sedimentary rock. A shallow sea once covered this part of the Great Plains, and most of the rock is soft sedimentary stuff like red sandstone and siltstone, with a little shale mixed in. The flat-topped cone that became Devils Tower used to be under that sea, but once the waters had receded, centuries of erosion gradually wore away the softer rock around the igneous cone, leaving it exposed. Today the cone thrusts 1,267 feet above the surrounding pine trees and prairie grasslands. That flat top no doubt gave Spielberg the idea of an extraterrestrials' spaceport; a parachutist did land on top in 1941, drawing great publicity—especially because he then had to figure out how to get down! Vertical cracks groove the sides of the tower in almost parallel columns, giving it its distinctive furrowed look. It's well-nigh irresistible for climbers, although you must register at the visitor center before attempting to ascend and follow strict regulations about bolts and drills. In deference to the Native American reverence for this sacred place, the park's staff urges climbers to voluntarily forego climbing in June, a month with many religious ceremonies for the local tribes.

For most of us, the best way to experience Devils Tower is to take the 1.3-mile paved **Tower Trail** that circles around the base. It's very kid-friendly, being mostly flat (after a steep climb at the start), with benches and interpretive stations along the way. Take your time walking so that you can examine this rugged pinnacle from every angle and in different lights. Bring sketchbooks and try to draw its stern majesty. And don't be surprised if the kids start mounding their mashed potatoes at dinner that night, tracing ridges on the sides with their forks . . .

While you're here, kids shouldn't miss the prairie dog towns on the park's east road, where black-tailed prairie dogs scamper about, popping in and out of their subterranean condos. You came out here to see the West—well, this is about as Western as it gets.

ⓘ Off U.S. 14 (✆ **307/467-5283;** www.nps.gov/deto).

✈ Gillette–Campbell County, 40 miles.

🛏 $$ **Hotel Alex Johnson,** 523 6th St., Rapid City, SD (✆ **800/ 888-2539** or 605/342-1210; www.alexjohnson.com). $$ **Sylvan Lake Lodge,** 24572 SD 87 (at SD 89), Custer, SD (✆ **888/875-0001** or 605/574-2561; www.custerresorts.com).

WHY THEY'LL THANK YOU: An icon of the West with mystical power.

Mystical Landscapes

5

Arches National Park
Sculpted by Nature
All ages • Moab, Utah

MORE THAN 2,000 IMPOSING NATURAL STONE ARCHES PUNCTUATE this sandstone plateau, almost as if it were one gigantic pop-up book. These are natural formations, the result of cycles of freezing and thawing rain and snow that continually dissolve the "glue" that holds together the sand grains of the stone, chipping away at them bit by bit over time. And yet, knowing the scientific process doesn't detract from the marvel of it, a seemingly endless variety of shapes and delicate colors, as if some giant sculptor were deliberately trying to make each arch more fantastic than the one before.

It's a place to let your imagination go wild. Is **Delicate Arch** really so delicate, or would its other nicknames (Old Maids Bloomers or Cowboy Chaps) be more appropriate? And what about those tall spires? You might imagine they're castles, the towering masts of stone sailing ships, or the petrified skyscrapers of some ancient city. Be sure to pick up a map at the visitor center, because half the fun is matching up the formations with the fanciful names that have been given to them. On the 18-mile scenic drive from one end of the park to the other, you'll pass such features as **Park Avenue,** a solid rock "fin" that reminded somebody of the Manhattan skyline; the **La Sal Mountains,** which early explorers thought looked like piles of salt; **Courthouse Towers,** with such monoliths as **Sheep Rock, The Organ,** and **The Three Gossips;** and the **Tower of Babel.** A side road leads to **The Windows, Turret Arch,** and the

Delicate Arch in Arches National Park, Utah.

Cove of Caves, where erosion is even now slowly making a new arch out of the largest cave. Detour onto **Wolfe Ranch Road** for a brief hike to see a 100-year-old ranch and some **Ute pictographs.**

Along the drive, stop to venture onto the various walking trails, many of them short and easy enough for even young children. A .3-mile walk lets you circle **Balanced Rock,** a 3,000-ton boulder perched on a slowly eroding pedestal; a .5-mile there-and-back trail leads past the **Parade of Elephants** to **Double Arch;** and another .3-mile walk goes to **Sand Dune Arch,** with an irresistible sandy hollow beneath that the kids can play in.

(**i**) U.S. 191 (© **435/719-2299;** www.nps.gov/arch).

✈ Grand Junction Regional, CO, 125 miles. Salt Lake City International, UT, 230 miles.

🏨 $ **Arch View Resort RV Camp Park,** U.S. 191 & UT 313 (© **800/813-6622** or 435/259-7854; www.archviewresort.com). $$ **Bowen Motel,** 169 N. Main St. (© **800/874-5439** or 435/259-7132; www.bowenmotel.com).

WHY THEY'LL THANK YOU: Waiting for Balanced Rock to topple.

Mystical Landscapes

6

Petrified Forest & Painted Desert
Trees of Stone, Stones of Color
All ages • Near Holbrook, Arizona

FROM THE NAME, CHILDREN MAY EXPECT TO SEE STANDING TREES OF stone, leaves and branches and all. Well, a better name for the **Petrified Forest** might be the Petrified Pile of Logs, with its fossilized hunks of ancient trees scattered like kindling across the arid scrubby landscape. But these richly colored petrifactions are plenty impressive close up, and the other half of the park, the **Painted Desert,** more than lives up to its name, in glowing pastel beauty. And now the park is bigger than ever: A deal signed by the National Park Service in September 2011 expanded Petrified Forest Park by roughly a quarter of its previous size to include land that scientists suspect could contain valuable archaeological sites—stay tuned.

Start your visit at the **Rainbow Forest Museum,** the visitor center at the southern entrance to the park, where the displays will teach the kids how those petrified logs got petrified in the first place. These 225-million-year-old conifers date from the late Triassic age, when this area was an equatorial tropical forest. The trees fell, were buried in sediment, and then were overlaid with volcanic ash, which gradually deposited silica in the trees that replaced their cells with quartz crystals. This unique set of circumstances left a profusion of these immense fossils in the area, which were sliced up and sold for souvenirs at such a rate that, in 1906, the government stepped in to preserve what was left in this park. A short

The Painted Desert.

walking trail behind the visitor center winds around a hillside strewn with logs (4–5 ft. in diameter), giving the children a first chance to examine them up close; across the road, a 2-mile loop takes you to **Agate House,** a ruined pueblo fashioned out of colorful petrified wood.

Once you're back in the car, head north on the park's 27-mile scenic road. Several overlooks highlight wonders such as the **Crystal Forest** (unfortunately, tourists pried the quartz and amethyst crystals out of these logs long ago); the **Jasper Forest,** petrified trees with their roots still attached; and **Agate Bridge,** a natural bridge formed by a petrified log. In the hazy blue badlands of the **Blue Mesa,** chunks of petrified wood teeter on mounds of soft clay that are eroding away beneath them. The Teepees are a lovely set of hills striped with different colors. At **Newspaper Rock,** you can gaze upon ancient **Native-American petroglyphs,** with the ruined pueblos of their creators at nearby **Pueblo Parco.**

Across I-40, you'll be fully in the **Painted Desert** section of the park, where a series of eight overlooks lets you admire the breathtaking desert colors, which were caused by various minerals in the mudstone-and-clay soil—iron, manganese, and others—which oxidized at different rates as they were exposed by erosion. It's a dreamscape of pastels washing over dramatically eroded buttes and mesas, one of nature's best special effects ever.

ⓘ U.S. 180, 20 miles east of Holbrook (✆ **928/524-6228;** www. nps.gov/pefo).

✈ Flagstaff Pulliam, 90 miles. Phoenix Sky Harbor International, 180 miles.

🛏 $$$ **La Posada,** 303 E. Second St., Winslow (✆ **928/289-4366;** www.laposada.org). $ **Wigwam Motel,** 811 W. Hopi Dr., Holbrook (✆ **928/524-3048;** www.galerie-kokopelli.com/wigwam).

WHY THEY'LL THANK YOU: If the rock logs don't get them, the Kodachrome mesas will.

Hawaii Volcanoes National Park
Where Hot Lava Still Flows
Ages 6 & up • Volcano, Hawaii

HAWAII VOLCANOES NATIONAL PARK BEATS OUT ALL THE OTHER U.S. national parks on two scores: It has the only tropical rainforest, and it has the only active volcano. Since 1983, the Big Island's **Kilauea volcano** has been erupting regularly, although these are "quiet" eruptions, with gas escaping slowly instead of exploding violently. Its slow-moving red lava oozes over the landscape, sometimes even over the park roads. The kids may wish they could see volcanic fireworks, but once they're here, feeling the soles of their sneakers getting gummy from the heat below, they'll realize this is spectacular enough.

This is not a tame volcano, not by any means. Over the past 2 decades, some $100 million worth of property has been destroyed by the eruptions, though the lava flow has also added 560 acres of new land. On many days, the lava flows right alongside accessible roads and you can get as close as the heat will allow. Thanks to sulfur dioxide gas from a new vent that opened in **Halemaumau Crater** in March 2008, a section of the park's **Crater Rim Drive** is currently closed to visitors. You can still see a large portion of the park, however, including the fuming vent (from a safe distance), and most kids will be excited at the chance to experience nature in action.

Near the visitor center, you can get your first glimpse of **Kilauea Caldera**, a 2½-mile-wide, 500-foot-deep pit with wisps of steam rising from it. Going counterclockwise on Crater Rim Road, you'll drive past the **Sulphur Banks,** which smell like rotten eggs, and the **Steam Vents,** fissures where trails of smoke, once molten lava, escape from the inner reaches of the earth. At the **Thomas A. Jaggar Museum,** there's a viewpoint for **Halemaumau Crater,** which is half a mile across but 1,000 feet deep; in 2008, a new fuming vent opened in this long-dormant fire pit, which can be viewed safely from the museum overlook. Near the **Iki Crater,** the .5-mile **Devastation Trail** is a sobering look at how a volcanic eruption wreaked havoc in 1959. Another intriguing stop is the **Thurston Lava Tube,** a cool underground hole in a lush forested bowl that somehow escaped the lava flow.

By now you won't be surprised to learn that the volcano goddess, Pele, was an important deity to ancient Hawaiians—you definitely wanted to be on the right side of this lady. At the 15-mile mark down **Chain of Craters Road,** you can see **Puu Loa,** an ancient site sacred to the Hawaiians, where a 2-mile boardwalk

The rugged, unforgiving landscape of Volcanoes National Park.

loop trail will show you thousands of mysterious Hawaiian petroglyphs carved in stone.

If the volcano is actively erupting, call the visitor center for directions to the best locations for night viewing—it's quite a sight, watching as the brilliant red lava snakes down the side of the mountain and pours into the cold sea, hissing and steaming ferociously. Of course, the ultimate view is from the sky: **Blue Hawaiian Helicopter** (📞 **800/745-BLUE** or 808/961-5600; www.bluehawaiian. com) runs several tours right over the bubbling caldera, for a bird's-eye view you'll never forget.

ⓘ Hawaii Belt Rd. (Hwy. 11; 📞 **808/985-6000;** www.nps.gov/havo).

✈ Hilo International, 29 miles.

🛏 $$ **Kilauea Lodge,** Old Volcano Rd., off Hwy. 11 (📞 **808/967-7366;** www.kilauealodge.com).

WHY THEY'LL THANK YOU: Red-hot magma.

Niagara Falls
The Big Spill
All ages • New York, USA & Ontario, Canada

EVERYONE'S SEEN A KODACHROME PHOTO OF **NIAGARA FALLS,** THAT stupendous curve of cascading water that lies between the United States and Canada. It's one of those sites, however, to which postcards will never do justice: To stand on a viewing platform and see, really see, how big it is, to hear the thunder of falling water, to feel the mist spritzing your face and the earth shaking under your feet, is another thing altogether. Kids don't understand how amazing it is until they're actually there.

There are actually two waterfalls here, both of them doozies: the **American Falls** and **Horseshoe Falls.** Both are around 175 feet high, although Horseshoe Falls, at 2,500 feet wide, is more than twice as wide as its sibling. The Canadian shore has the real panoramic view; both falls can be seen from the American side, but not together (Prospect Point for the American Falls, Terrapin Point for Horseshoe Falls). The Canadian side tends to have better hotels and more attractions as well. No matter where you stay, you can easily visit both, by crossing the **Rainbow Bridge,** preferably on foot—it's only the length of a couple city blocks. Bring a passport (or a driver's license and original birth certificate; you'll need birth certificates for the kids as well).

On the U.S. shore, head for **Niagara Falls State Park** (✆ 716/278-1796; www.niagarafallsstatepark.com) to explore the falls: An **Observation Tower** overlooks the river, and the **Cave of the Winds tour** (Apr–Oct; ✆ 716/278-1730) takes you by elevator down onto boardwalks, where you can walk around the base of the American Falls. Canada's 775-foot-high **Skylon Tower,** 5200 Robinson St. (✆ 905/356-2651; www.skylon.com), has a revolving restaurant on top, and the **Journey Behind the Falls** (✆ 905/354-1551; www.niagaraparks.com) allows you to descend via elevator to tunnels punctuated with portholes that look out through the blur

15

The American Falls.

of water right behind Horseshoe Falls. The coolest way to see the falls, of course, is the classic ***Maid of the Mist* boat ride** (Apr–Oct; ☎ 716/284-8897; www.maidofthemist.com), which plays no favorites; it departs from either shore. You'll chug upriver toward the American and Horseshoe Falls, sailing right up the base of both (don't worry, blue slickers are provided to keep you dry).

Want more of an adrenaline rush? Book a 10-minute helicopter ride over the cascades with **Niagara Helicopters** (☎ **905/357-5672;** www.niagarahelicopters.com) or **Rainbow Air** (☎ **716/284-2800;** www.rainbowairinc.com), or crash through the white waters of the Niagara gorge with **Whirlpool Jet Boat Tours** (Apr–Oct; ☎ **888/438-4444** in the U.S., or 905/468-4800 in Canada; www.whirlpooljet.com). This being a major tourist destination, there's a ton of other attractions around, from historic old forts and botanical gardens to aquariums and amusement parks. But overdeveloped as it may be, the spectacular Falls are still there.

ⓘ U.S. (ⓒ **877/FALLSUS** [325-5787] or 716/282-8992; www.niagara-usa.com). Canada (ⓒ **800/563-2557** or 905/356-6061; www.niagarafallstourism.com).

✈ Buffalo Niagara International, 34km (21 miles).

🛏 $$ **Courtyard by Marriott,** 5950 Victoria Ave., Niagara Falls, Ontario, Canada (ⓒ **800/771-1123** or 905/358-3083; www.nfcourtyard.com). $$$ **Red Coach Inn,** 2 Buffalo Ave., Niagara Falls, NY, USA (ⓒ **866/719-2070** or 716/282-1459; www.redcoach.com).

BEST TIME: May to October.

WHY THEY'LL THANK YOU: Roaring water, mist, and rainbows galore.

 Train Rides

Durango & Silverton Narrow Gauge Railroad
Classic Steam Train
All ages • Durango, Colorado

EVER SINCE IT WAS BUILT IN 1882, THIS LITTLE TRAIN HAS BEEN PUFFing along the Rio de las Animas Perdidas (that's Spanish for the River of Lost Souls, a haunting name indeed), traveling 45 miles through the mountains and San Juan National Forest to the town of Silverton and back. When it was first built, Silverton was, as its name suggests, a silver-mining town, and the train's business was to bring precious ore back down to the railroad hub of Durango. When the United States went on the gold standard in 1893, the price of silver dropped dramatically, throwing this region's economy into a tailspin. Many local railroads went belly up, but this one survived because of its incredible scenic views. Nowadays, it's tourists that trundle along those tracks, in strings of restored gold-colored Victorian-era coaches.

The Durango & Silverton Narrow Gauge Railroad.

Traveling at around 18 mph, you'll climb 3,000 feet, past relics of the area's mining and railroading activities; elevations en route range from 8,000 feet at the passes to 14,000 feet on the peaks you'll see from the train windows. White puffs of smoke trail from its coal-powered steam locomotives—a fireman shovels about 6 tons of coal per day to power these locomotives. If you look at the tracks, they're only 3 feet apart (standard train tracks are 4 ft. 8½ in. wide), which makes it easier to navigate sharp mountain curves. In this train's case, however, the narrower tracks also meant workers had fewer inches to cut out of the sheer granite cliff face of the Animas Gorge. Good thing, too—it was already such a risky job that the railroad's president, William Palmer, constructed the route in secret, fearing that the directors of the Denver & Rio Grande Railroad would veto the plan before he could safely complete it.

This is a full-day excursion—it takes 3½ hours to ride from Durango to Silverton, you're given 2 hours to poke around picturesque Victorian-era Silverton, and then it's another 3½ hours back down to Durango. (Before getting on the train in Durango, you could also spend half an hour or so in the attached **D&SNG Museum,** right beside the train depot.) You'll have a couple of hours to explore Silverton before the return trip; one fun thing to do is to visit the **Old Hundred Gold Mine** (© **800/872-3009** or 970/387-5444; www.minetour.com) in Cunningham Pass, just outside of Silverton. The tour takes you a third of a mile deep into **Galena Mountain** on an electric mine car, where miners demonstrate historic mining equipment and techniques. There's also gold panning, and box lunches are included in the deal.

The views are even more spectacular on the ride back. In fact, the stretch of U.S. 550 that parallels the train tracks is called the **Million-Dollar Highway,** not only because it was so expensive to build, but because you'll get million-dollar Rocky Mountain views all the way home.

ⓘ 479 Main Ave. (© **877/872-4607** or 970/247-2733; www. durangotrain.com).

✈ Durango–La Plata County, 14 miles.

🛏 $$ Strater Hotel, 699 Main Ave., Durango (© **800/247-4431** or 970/247-4431; www.strater.com).

WHY THEY'LL THANK YOU: Clinging to the cliff face.

10 Boat Rides

The Seattle-Victoria Ferry
Sailing the High-Speed Puget Cats
All ages • Seattle, Washington, USA, to Victoria, British Columbia, Canada

CROSSING THE U.S.-CANADA BORDER IS GENERALLY A FAIRLY ROUTINE experience—but not if you sail across it on a high-speed catamaran from Seattle, Washington, to Victoria, British Columbia. The trip takes only 3 hours, just enough time for the kids to roam around the boat, get a bite to eat, and stare out the windows at the gorgeous northwest coast. Exciting as open water is, it soon gets monotonous for children; one of the glories of this trip for kids is that most of the ride is on glacier-carved **Puget Sound,** where land can be viewed on either side, the rugged conifer-mantled highlands of the Olympic Peninsula on one side and the rural Skagit Valley on the other.

You leave from Seattle's busy ferry port, Pier 69, with the futuristic Space Needle lifting its curious head over the downtown Seattle skyline and majestic Mount Rainier visible to the south, snowcapped even in summer. Working your way past the harbor's sailboat and kayak traffic, you'll enter convoluted Puget Sound, with the mountains of the Olympic Peninsula gradually rearing their peaks on your left. Coming out of Puget Sound near Port Townsend, you'll see the lovely **San Juan Islands** on the right (the same company runs ferries to the San Juans, including some whale-watching excursions). Then it's across the **Strait of Juan de Fuca,** the first stretch of open water on your voyage so far.

On the far side of that strait lies Vancouver—**Vancouver Island,** that is, which is not the same thing as the mainland city of Vancouver. What is on Vancouver Island is British Columbia's capital, **Victoria,** which is like a little slice of Victorian England served up on the northwest coast of North America. Ferry schedules are organized to make a day trip perfectly doable, with plenty of time to explore Victoria before heading back to Seattle. The mild Pacific climate is beautifully suited to horticulture, and Victoria's pride and joy is its rose gardens, particularly the spectacular **Butchart Gardens,** 800 Benvenuto Ave., Brentwood Bay (© **866/652-4422** or 250/652-4422; www.butchartgardens.com). If you can't sell your kids on visiting a garden, there's plenty to see around the charmingly restored Inner Harbour: **Miniature World,** in the Fairmont Empress Hotel, 649 Humboldt St. (© **250/385-9731;** www.miniatureworld.com), with loads of small-scale dioramas from history and literature; the glass-enclosed views of harbor creatures in the **Pacific Undersea Gardens,** 490 Belleville St. (© **250/382-5717;** www.pacificunderseagardens.com); and the **Victoria Butterfly Gardens,** 1461 Benvenuto Ave., Brentwood Bay (© **877/722-0272** or 250/652-3822; www.butterflygardens.com), which are exactly what the name says.

(i) Victoria Clipper Ferries (© **800/888-2535,** 206/448-5000, or 250/382-8100; www.clippervacations.com).

✈ Seattle-Tacoma International/Victoria International.

🛏 $$ **Admiral Inn,** 257 Belleville St., Victoria (© **888/823-6472** or 250/388-6267; www.admiral.bc.ca). $$$ **The Edgewater,** Pier 67, 2411 Alaskan Way, Seattle (© **800/624-0670** or 206/728-7000; www.edgewaterhotel.com).

WHY THEY'LL THANK YOU: Gliding up the fjord in time for tea and scones.

11 Boat Rides

Cruising the Mighty Mississippi
A River Ride Through the Heart of America
All ages • Various locations along the Mississippi River

THE NATIVE AMERICANS LIVING ON ITS SHORES CALLED IT THE Messipi, or "big river," but in American lore the Mississippi River is so much more. Yes, it is long—at 2,350 miles, it's the third-longest river in the world—but as it surges north to south down the middle of America, it gives this continent a heartbeat that is essentially, uniquely ours. I vividly remember the thrill of crossing it for the first time, at age 13, on a nighttime train, with a momentous feeling of Heading West. To ride its majestic brown waters, for whatever stretch of the river, is to feel connected to West and East and North and South all at once.

Thanks to Mark Twain's depiction of the river in such books as *The Adventures of Tom Sawyer, The Adventures of Huckleberry Finn,* and *Life on the Mississippi,* most Americans envision the Mississippi as a huge, muddy brown river, rolling powerfully between its banks. That's what the river looks like south of St. Louis, in the Missouri area where Twain grew up. But the Mississippi is born much farther north, in Lake Itasca, Minnesota, where it's a much meeker and milder river indeed. After it merges with the Minnesota River at St. Anthony Falls, the Upper Mississippi becomes a more dramatic waterway, cutting its majestic course between steep river bluffs. You can explore this section of the river on an overnight cruise between the Iowa cities of LeClaire and Dubuque on the **Riverboat _Twilight_** (© **800/331-1467** or 815/845-2333; www. riverboattwilight.com). Though you'll stay overnight in accommodations on shore, you'll spend your days on the decks of this ornate replica sternwheeler, with smokestacks and lacy white fretwork and live traditional folk and country music to set the mood.

In Dubuque, don't miss visiting the **National Mississippi River Museum & Aquarium** (350 E. 3rd St.; © **800/226-3369** or 563/557-9545; www.rivermuseum.com)—it has lots of interactive exhibits to help kids understand the river's flood patterns, geography, and history. If their attention flags, switch over to the connected aquarium to see giant catfish and bayou alligators and other river denizens.

Of course, you can also drive the **Great River Road Scenic Byway**, a national historic highway that follows the river's course for some 3,000 miles through its ten states. Along the way, several river towns offer 1- or 2-hour paddle-wheel cruises to give you a taste of what it feels like to be out on that great river—St. Paul, Minnesota; La Crosse, Wisconsin; St. Louis, Missouri; Memphis, Tennessee; Vicksburg, Mississippi; and New Orleans, Louisiana all have sightseeing paddle-wheelers. Memphis even has a scale model of the river, constructed in **Mud Island River Park** (125 N. Front St.; © **800/507-6507** or 901/576-7241; www.mudisland. com). That'll bring "Ol' Man River" home to the kids for sure.

ⓘ www.experiencemississippiriver.com.

✈ Depends on port of embarkation.

⇌ Included in cruise packages.

WHY THEY'LL THANK YOU: Rolling down the river.

Scouting Alaska's Inside Passage

Ferries to the Glacier

All ages • Juneau, Alaska

EVERY SUMMER, BOATLOADS OF TOURISTS CROWD ONTO LUXURY cruise ships to be pampered on their way through Alaska. But that's not my idea of a rugged wilderness experience—not when you can still travel in comfort on the swift, well-outfitted ferries of the Alaska Marine Highway System, with the option of planning your own itinerary to suit your family's interests.

Officially designated an **All-American Road,** the Alaska Marine Highway covers 3,500 nautical miles from Bellingham, Washington, out to the Aleutian Islands. A fleet of sleek blue-hulled ferries steams its entire length, but I think the most interesting segments are those of the **Inside Passage,** that crazy network of inlets and channels around the countless islands of the Alaskan Panhandle. Squeezed between the Canadian Yukon and the Gulf of Alaska, this strip of southeast Alaska—a breathtaking mix of dense green northwest rainforest and pristine white glaciers—stretches 500 miles from Ketchikan to Yakutat.

In the middle is Juneau, Alaska's capital city and where you'll probably arrive by plane. Before leaving Juneau, trundle the kids off to see the **Mendenhall Glacier,** Glacier Spur Road (✆ **907/789-0097**), where you can stand in front of a wall of blue ice and feel its chilly breath. The two destinations that most interest my kids are **Ketchikan,** a spruced-up logging town, with the world's largest collection of totem poles, that's 19 hours south of Juneau by ferry; and **Sitka,** an exotic mix of Russian and Tlingit cultures, that's 9 hours south of Juneau by ferry.

Spending several hours on these ferries is no problem. These are handsome modern craft, with restaurants, gift shops, and in some cases even movie theaters, not to mention solariums and observation lounges where you can park yourselves to watch the scenic coast roll past. Naturalists often come along for the ride to talk about Alaska's wildlife and geology with passengers; some ships have small video arcades or play areas for toddlers. For overnight journeys, you can reserve two- to four-berth cabins (book several months in advance for summer voyages), although you are also free to roll out your sleeping bags on the comfy reclining seats in the lounges. Hey, that counts as roughing it in my book.

(i) **Alaska Marine Highway System** (© **800/642-0066** or 907/465-3941; www.dot.state.ak.us/amhs).

✈ Juneau International.

🛏 $$ **The Driftwood Lodge,** 435 Willoughby Ave., Juneau (© **800/544-2239** or 907/586-2280; www.driftwoodalaska.com). $$$ **Goldbelt Hotel,** 51 Egan Dr., Juneau (© **888/478-6909** or 907/586-6900; www.goldbelttours.com).

WHY THEY'LL THANK YOU: Waking up to see a glacier slide past your window.

Super City Parks **13**

Boston Common
New England's Ultimate Town Green
All ages • Boston, Massachusetts

THE OLDEST PUBLIC PARK IN THE UNITED STATES, TREE-STREWN **Boston Common** (bordered by Beacon, Park, Tremont, Boylston, and Charles sts.) slopes confidently down from the prim mansions of Beacon Hill to the skyscrapers of downtown, overlooked by the gold dome of the State House. In colonial days, it was at various times a public cow pasture, gallows site, and British army encampment; today it bustles with picnickers, Frisbee and softball games, kite flyers, and busking musicians. The Frog Pond, where there really were frogs at one time, makes a pleasant spot to splash around in the summer and skate in the winter.

Many visitors confuse the rambling Common with its neighbor, the more sprucely landscaped **Public Garden,** the country's first botanical garden, where the famous swan boats glide over a man-made pond and a popular set of bronze statues commemorate the classic children's book *Make Way for Ducklings*. The Public Garden is lovely, yes, but there's something quintessentially American about Boston Common, despite the occasional bald patches of ground.

At the Boylston Street side, the **Central Burying Ground** contains the grave of famed portraitist Gilbert Stuart, and free concerts and plays are held at the nearby **Parkman Bandstand.** The aristo-cratic brick town houses of **Beacon Hill** overlook the Common along its north side, and the gold dome of the State House presides over the east end (note the eccentric codfish weather vane on top). On the Beacon Street edge of the Common, across from the State House, a stunning **memorial** designed by Augustus Saint-Gaudens

Boston Common.

honors Bostonian Col. Robert Gould Shaw and the Union Army's 54th Massachusetts Colored Regiment, the first American army unit made up of free black soldiers, celebrated in the 1989 movie *Glory*. And lest we get too historic, we should also mention the irresistibly touristy **Cheers,** 84 Beacon St. (✆ **617/227-9605;** www. cheersboston.com), originally the Bull & Finch Pub (a replica of the TV set is at Faneuil Hall Marketplace).

The Common is, appropriately enough, the starting point for the **Freedom Trail** (✆ **617/357-8300;** www.thefreedomtrail.org), a historic 3-mile walking route (follow a red line painted on the sidewalks); maps are available at the **visitor information booth** at 148 Tremont St. My kids enjoy its connect-the-dots approach to sightseeing every bit as much as I did as a child. A hard-core history fiend can easily spend 4 hours along the trail, but a family with restless children can easily do it in less—especially since you can quit at any point. (Just don't miss the **Paul Revere House,** at 19 North Sq., one of my childhood favorites.)

ⓘ **Greater Boston Convention & Visitors Bureau,** 2 Copley Place (✆ **888/SEE-BOSTON** [733-2678] or 617/536-4100; www. bostonusa.com), or **City of Boston** (✆ **617/357-8300;** www. cityofboston.gov/FreedomTrail/bostoncommon.asp).

✈ Boston Logan International.

🛏 $$ **DoubleTree Suites by Hilton,** 400 Soldiers Field Rd. (✆ **800/222-TREE** [8733] or 617/783-0090; www.doubletree.com). $ **The Midtown Hotel,** 220 Huntington Ave. (✆ **800/343-1177** or 617/262-1000; www.midtownhotel.com).

WHY THEY'LL THANK YOU: Picnicking and frolicking in the shadow of 3½ centuries of history.

Escape to Alcatraz
America's Most Famous Prison
Ages 8 & up • San Francisco, California

WHAT DO YOU DO WITH THE MOST NOTORIOUS HARDENED CRIMINALS in the federal prison system? In 1934, at the height of the gangster era, the government had a brainstorm: Wall them up in a converted military fort on an island in San Francisco Bay surrounded by sheer cliffs, frigid waters, and treacherous currents. Just let them *try* to escape from there. Thus was the **Alcatraz Island federal penitentiary** born, a maximum-security prison whose infamous inmates included Al Capone, "Machine Gun" Kelly, and Robert Stroud (the Birdman). You may recognize its impregnable profile, lit by an ominous domed beacon tower, from such movies as *The Birdman of Alcatraz*, *Escape from Alcatraz*, and *The Rock*; it hasn't held a prisoner since 1963, but the vibe is still eerie—and therefore irresistible to youngsters.

The cell of Robert Stroud, aka the "Birdman of Alcatraz."

These days it's harder to get into Alcatraz than it is to get out of it, thanks to the popularity of National Park Service tours to the island; call at least a month in advance to reserve tickets. You'll take a ferry from Fisherman's Wharf and explore the famous prison with a slide show and audio tour, which includes fascinating stories told by former guards and inmates. As you listen to the audio narration and the grim anecdotes delivered by park rangers, you get a chilling sense of what it was like to be isolated in the middle of the bay—with winds blustering through the barred windows and armed guards pacing the gun galley—yet so achingly close to the beautiful city of San Francisco.

By declaring Alcatraz to be "inescapable," the government was almost daring prisoners to break out. Officially, no one ever did, although there were 14 audacious attempts over the years: 23 fugitives were caught, 6 were shot, 2 drowned, and 5 others were missing and presumed drowned.

The ferry ride across the bay is fun, but you'll want to wear jackets, even in summer—and wear comfortable shoes, because there are many stairs to climb. Older kids who want to ratchet up the tour's already somber tone may opt for the even spookier evening tour. Hey, if you're going for creepy, you might as well go all the way.

ⓘ www.nps.gov/alcatraz or **Alcatraz Cruises,** Pier 33 (© **415/ 981-7625;** www.alcatrazcruises.com). **San Francisco Municipal Transportation Agency** (www.sfmta.com). **San Francisco Travel Association,** 900 Market St. (© **415/391-2000;** www.sanfrancisco. travel).

✈ San Francisco International, 13 miles. Oakland International, 18 miles.

🛏 $$$ **Argonaut Hotel,** 495 Jefferson St. (© **866/415-0704** or 415/563-0800; www.argonauthotel.com). $$ **Larkspur Hotel,** 524 Sutter St. (© **866/823-4669** or 415/421-2865; www.larkspurhotel unionsquare.com).

WHY THEY'LL THANK YOU: Appreciating the sweet taste of freedom.

Mount Rushmore & the Crazy Horse Memorial

All ages • Keystone & Custer, South Dakota

WHEN YOU THINK ABOUT IT, MOUNT RUSHMORE IS ONE OF THE ODDEST monuments ever: Gigantic chiseled faces of four presidents—why four? Why those four (Washington, Jefferson, Lincoln, and . . . Theodore Roosevelt)? And why in the South Dakota badlands, miles away from most U.S. citizens? But crazy as it is, darned if another group didn't raise money to carve another mountain nearby with an even bigger sculpture, depicting American Indian chief **Crazy Horse.**

Mount Rushmore was the passion of one individual: Gutzon Borglum, a Danish-American sculptor from Idaho, who was hired by South Dakota to make a memorial to draw visitors to the Black Hills. Borglum—who had previously been hired to carve Stone Mountain in Georgia, until negotiations broke down—chose this peak because it was hard granite, the highest in the area, and it faced southeast, where it would catch good daytime light. He also picked which presidents to portray: Teddy Roosevelt made the cut because he'd lived in South Dakota and was a conservationist (also because Borglum had already done a bust of T.R. for the U.S. Capitol). The project was conceived in 1923; sculpting began in 1927 and puttered along through the Depression. Washington was unveiled in 1934, Jefferson in 1936, Lincoln in 1937, and Roosevelt in 1939. Borglum died in 1941, and though his son Lincoln continued for 7 months, the work halted for good when the U.S. entered World War II.

Visit the **museum** under the amphitheater to learn about Borglum's innovative engineering. A 1-mile **Presidential Trail** leads to viewing terraces at the base of the mountain; take a guided tour so the kids can learn all the curious history. It's great to catch Mount Rushmore by the dawn's early light, or at least as soon as the park opens at 8am. In summer, a nightly lighting ceremony at 9pm (8pm mid-Aug to Sept) makes another splendid viewing op.

Mount Rushmore.

To many Native Americans, Mount Rushmore is a sacrilege, an intrusion on sacred landscapes, so the Lakota tribe initiated their own project 17 miles away, hiring sculptor Korczak Ziolkowski, who'd briefly worked with Borglum on Mount Rushmore. He began to hew the image of Chief Crazy Horse astride a thundering stallion in 1948; 50 years later—16 years after Ziolkowski himself had died—only the chief's nine-story-high face was completed. While the sculpture is still a work in progress, millions of tons of rock have been blasted from the mountain face, and even kids should be able to trace the form emerging from the granite; nightly laser shows in summer project the finished design onto the rough-hewn rock. When finished, Crazy Horse will be so big that all four heads on Mount Rushmore can fit inside it—641 feet long and 563 feet high. At the base of the mountain, the **Indian Museum of North America** focuses on the tribal history of numerous Native American cultures.

ⓘ **Mount Rushmore National Memorial,** SD 244, Keystone (ⓒ **605/574-2523;** www.nps.gov/moru). **Crazy Horse Memorial,** U.S. 16/385, north of Custer (ⓒ **605/673-4681;** www.crazyhorse.org).

✈ Rapid City Regional, 35 miles.

🛏 $$ **Hotel Alex Johnson,** 523 6th St., Rapid City (✆ **800/888-2539** or 605/342-1210; www.alexjohnson.com). $$ **Sylvan Lake Lodge,** 24572 SD 87 (at SD 89), Custer (✆ **888/875-0001** or 605/574-2561; www.custerresorts.com).

WHY THEY'LL THANK YOU: Giant statues for American giants.

<table>
<tr><td>**16**</td><td>A Touch of Kitsch</td></tr>
</table>

Wall Drug
The Power of Advertising
All ages • Wall, South Dakota

AT THE OTHER END OF SOUTH DAKOTA'S I-90 CORRIDOR FROM THE Corn Palace, **Wall Drug** is a one-of-a-kind phenomenon—a wayside stop that just kept growing and growing. It all began in the Depression, when nearby Mount Rushmore was still under scaffolding, years away from attracting travelers to this middle-of-nowhere burg. Desperate for business, Wall Drug's owners, Ted and Dorothy Hustead, put up signs on the highway advertising free ice water to thirsty travelers. Motorists poured in.

Now convinced of the power of advertising, the Husteads planted more and more billboards, until they even began to appear in foreign countries. The Highway Beautification Act of the 1960s severely limited Wall Drug's billboard campaign, but still the tourists came; and over the years the Husteads (who still own the place, though it's now in the hands of the third generation) have added more and more popular features to draw them in.

Some 20,000 people a day, it's estimated, pull off the road to mill around this shambling low-slung complex, so extensive that it scarcely seems like a drugstore anymore. (There is a replica of the original small pharmacy inside, however.) Along with a "mall" of 26 little shops, Wall Drug has a restaurant, a vast postcard store, a gallery selling Western art, displays of Native American artifacts, a mechanical diorama of an American Indian village, and a mocked-up Main Street of a Western town. But wait! There's more! Animated figures tucked into every available niche "speak" to the customers, including a roaring T-Rex. Out in the back yard stand king-size plaster figures of a bucking bronco, a rabbit, and the mythical jackalope, and an 80-foot-long green brontosaurus statue benignly casts its shade over the children's play area.

Nothing defines "tourist trap" better than Wall Drug. That's why you must visit.

(i) 510 Main St. (© **605/279-2175;** www.walldrug.com).

✈ Rapid City Regional, 55 miles.

🛏 $$ **Hotel Alex Johnson,** 523 6th St., Rapid City (© **800/888-2539** or 605/342-1210; www.alexjohnson.com). $$ **Sylvan Lake Lodge,** 24572 SD 87 (at SD 89), Custer (© **888/875-0001** or 605/574-2561; www.custerresorts.com).

WHY THEY'LL THANK YOU: Classic roadside Americana.

A Touch of Kitsch

17

The Corn Palace
Harvest Gone Wild

All ages • Mitchell, South Dakota

ON THAT CLASSIC COAST-TO-COAST SEE-AMERICA-FIRST DRIVE IN THE family truckster, once you hit the Great Plains things begin to seem a little slow—it's just such a long way between cities. That's the appeal of the **Corn Palace,** sitting right off South Dakota's long east–west stretch of I-90. You have to get off the road somewhere, and when you do, it might as well be somewhere that makes you blink your eyes in wonder.

Turning onto Mitchell's main street downtown, you can't miss the Corn Palace, a gaudy, multicolor riot of onion domes and turrets. It was originally built in 1921 as the main exposition hall for this agricultural market town, but in a way the Corn Palace is built new every year. Every spring, a different artist announces a theme and sets to work, creating a set of **murals** to cover the outside of the Corn Palace—murals made out of *corn*. Yes, that's right, kernels and husks of real corn are applied to the facade, a custom that goes back to the 1890s when the first Corn Palace was opened. Actually, it still seems bizarre, no matter how long they've been doing it. But that's why the Corn Palace looks as though it's made out of corn, though underneath the building is mere reinforced concrete.

Concerts, stage shows, and sports events take place in and out of the hall, and still the artists work to complete their design, using thousands of bushels of native South Dakota corn, grain, and grasses. Come here in the summer and you'll still see a work in progress.

If you are visiting in July, considering treating your kids to an authentic rodeo. The **Corn Palace Stampede Rodeo** is a 4-day event featuring top-notch competitors. There are tons of activities for kids of all ages. To learn more, check out their website at www.cornpalacestampede.com.

(i) 604 N. Main St. ((C) **866/273-CORN** [2676] or 605/996-6223; www.cornpalace.org).

✈ Sioux Falls Regional, 72 miles.

🛏 $$ **Days Inn,** 1506 S. Burr St. (I-90 & SD 37, Exit 332; (C) **888/440-2021** or 605/996-6208; www.daysinn.com).

WHY THEY'LL THANK YOU: It's beyond corny.

Winchester Mystery House
Monument to Paranoia

Ages 4 & up • San Jose, California

TRUTH CAN BE STRANGER THAN FICTION, AND NO THEME-PARK ATTRACTION could be any stranger than this actual house in San Jose, an hour's drive south of San Francisco. This quirky mansion, set in acres of meticulous gardens, was obviously the handiwork of a mad-woman. Walking through it on any of the various guided tours, you'll be astonished at its weird mix of luxury, good taste, and utter craziness.

Begun in 1884, the **Winchester Mystery House** is the legacy of Sarah L. Winchester, a 44-year-old widow. Her husband was the son of the famous rifle manufacturer Oliver Winchester, maker of the fabulously successful Winchester repeater rifle—sometimes called the "Gun That Won the West." After both her husband and her baby daughter died, the disconsolate Mrs. Winchester con-sulted with a seer, who proclaimed that the family lay under a special curse—targeted by the unhappy spirits of people who had been killed with Winchester rifles. Gullible Mrs. Winchester bought the idea, and that's when her personal tragedy took a peculiar twist. The medium told her those unquiet souls could be appeased by only one thing: perpetual construction on the Winchester man-sion. (Makes you wonder if she got a kickback from the contractor.) Convinced that she'd live as long as building continued, Mrs. Win-chester—who happened to have a fortune to spend on this scheme—went through most of her $20-million inheritance over the next 38 years, as construction work went on 24 hours a day, 7 days a week, 365 days a year.

As you can probably guess, this is no ordinary home. With **160 rooms,** it sprawls across half a dozen acres, a red-roofed Victorian mansion with extra turrets and gables sprouting randomly. There was never any master blueprint; Sarah Winchester herself designed the additions, often drawing them on a scrap of paper or a tablecloth whenever a new idea seized her. It has some 40 bedrooms, 47 fireplaces, and 5 kitchens, and a number of high-tech features for its time—elevators, forced-air heating, and gas light fixtures that could be turned on with the press of a button. Her favorite flower was the daisy, and it's fun to look for the **daisy motif** repeated in room after room.

Still, what kids undoubtedly remember most are the many disturbing features: a staircase leading nowhere, a Tiffany window with a spider-web design, a window in the floor, and doors that open onto blank walls. Superstitious Mrs. Winchester harped on the number 13, hoping thereby to confound the vengeful spirits—there are 13 bathrooms, 13 windows and doors in the old sewing room, 13 palms lining the main driveway, 13 hooks in the séance room, and chandeliers with 13 lights. Did the perpetual renovation plan work? Well, eventually Sarah Winchester did die, but not until the ripe old age of 82—with the house still unfinished, of course.

(i) 525 S. Winchester Blvd. (I-280 at CA 17; ✆ **408/247-2101;** www.winchestermysteryhouse.com).

✈ San Jose International, 5 miles. San Francisco International, 36 miles.

🛏 $$$ **Argonaut Hotel,** 495 Jefferson St., San Francisco (✆ **866/ 415-0704** or 415/563-0800; www.argonauthotel.com). $$ **Lark-spur Hotel,** 524 Sutter St., San Francisco (✆ **866/823-4669** or 415/421-2865; www.larkspurhotelunionsquare.com).

WHY THEY'LL THANK YOU: Realizing that even grown-ups get out of control sometimes.

Carlsbad Caverns
Colossal Underground Refuge

Ages 6 & up • Carlsbad, New Mexico

NATIVE AMERICANS ALWAYS KNEW THERE WAS A GIANT CAVE SYSTEM snaking around under the porous limestone reef of the Guadalupe Mountains. But white settlers only stumbled upon it a century ago, after noticing vast hordes of bats swarming out of a hole in the ground every summer day at sunset. Some 100 caves lie within today's park, an underground world of pale limestone, where every fantastic and grotesque shape imaginable (and unimaginable) has been sculpted by natural forces—from frozen waterfalls to strands of pearls, soda straws to miniature castles, draperies to ice-cream cones. Above all, what is impressive here is the sheer size of the cave, a constantly cool (56°F/13°C) refuge from the 100°F (38°C) heat outside in the Chihuahuan Desert.

The main cave open to the public, the immense **Carlsbad Cavern,** offers several options. With smaller kids, you may just want to take the elevator from the visitor center down 750 feet to the **Big Room,** which is a pretty understated name for this jaw-dropping rock chamber whose floor covers 14 acres. If you're more ambitious, follow the traditional explorer's route from the historic natural entrance, winding down for a mile into the depths through a series of underground rooms to the same Big Room. A self-guided tour from here runs 1¼ miles over a relatively level path, taking about an hour. Rangers along the path point out some of the more evocative formations, demonstrating the still-growing dome stalagmites and the daggerlike stalactites jabbing down from the ceiling.

Tours of other sections of Carlsbad Cavern range from the easy **Left Hand Tunnel,** a half-mile lantern tour, to the difficult **Hall of the White Giant,** which requires you to crawl long distances, squeeze through tight crevices, and climb up slippery flowstone-lined passages. The 2½-hour tour of **Slaughter Canyon Cave** is a far more strenuous cave hike from a different cave mouth

The Twin Domes in Carlsbad Caverns.

altogether, about a 45-minute drive from Carlsbad Caverns. (Visitors to Slaughter Canyon Cave will need to first pick up tickets at the Carlsbad Caverns Visitor Center.) And if the kids don't like being underground too long, they can still join one of the most popular activities at the caves, a sunset gathering at the natural entrance (May–Oct) to watch a quarter-million Mexican free-tailed bats flap out of the cavern to wheel out over the desert for a night of insect feasting. After all, that's how the cave was discovered in the first place.

ⓘ Carlsbad Caverns Visitor Center, 727 National Parks Hwy. (📞 **575/785-2232;** www.nps.gov/cave). Slaughter Canyon Cave, C.R. 418 turnoff from National Parks Hwy., Carlsbad.

✈ Cavern City, 23 miles. El Paso International, TX, 150 miles.

🛏 $$ **Rodeway Inn,** 6 Carlsbad Cavern Hwy., Whites City (📞 **800/CAVERNS** [228-3767] or 575/785-2296; www.rodewayinn. com).

WHY THEY'LL THANK YOU: The Big Room.

Famous Bridges

Bridges do more than connect two bits of land—they span centuries of history, ignite the imagination, and inspire with their beauty. Crossing a famous bridge becomes an event, a moment of drama that can crystallize your experience of a city. Natural spots for photo ops, bridges can thrill kids with a panoramic postcard view. Here are two of the greatest bridges in the U.S., sure to spark vivid family travel memories.

20 The Brooklyn Bridge, New York As thrilling a sight as this beautiful brown-hued East River bridge is from afar, with its Gothic-style towers and lacy mesh of cables, the view from the bridge is even more thrilling. A boardwalklike pedestrian walkway goes all the way across. One mile long, it should take half an hour to traverse—except you'll be tempted to stop more than once to ooh and ahh at the vision of **Manhattan's skyscrapers** thrusting upward, with the **great harbor** and **Verrazano-Narrows Bridge** beyond. The bridge took 16 years to build, from 1867 to 1883, becoming the first steel-wire suspension bridge in the world when it opened. (Until then, the only way to get from

In the Wild

22

Assateague
Island of the Wild Ponies
All ages • Assateague Island, Virginia

MISTY OF CHINCOTEAGUE IS ONE OF THOSE BOOKS MY DAUGHTER loved reading as much as I did—it's practically required reading for any girl in her Horse Phase. As every Misty lover knows, the book

Manhattan to Brooklyn was via ferry.) See Bronx Zoo ㉖, Statue of Liberty & Ellis Island ㊶, Metropolitan Museum of Art (61).

㉑ **The Golden Gate Bridge, San Francisco** Warn the kids ahead of time that the Golden Gate Bridge is not golden at all, but a flaming orange. Once past that surprise, though, they cannot fail to be bowled over by this glorious bridge spanning the Pacific Ocean where it meets San Francisco Bay. In all lights, it has a magical quality—brightening at dawn, glowing at sunset, glittering at night, or blazing proudly through the city's trademark fog. It's one of those quintessential landmarks, familiar from dozens of movies. Cars roll over it, boats cruise under it, and airplanes buzz overhead, but this bridge is best experienced on foot. Be prepared: The traffic alongside the pedestrian walkway gets pretty noisy, and the bridge vibrates, but if you make it to **Vista Point,** you'll be rewarded with a **breathtaking view.** See Escape to Alcatraz ⑭, the Exploratorium (52), and the Cable Cars of San Francisco (60). *http://goldengatebridge.org/visitors.*

is about a **Chincoteague pony,** and the place you go to see Chincoteague ponies is . . . **Assateague Island.** Chincoteague comes into the picture because it's the neighboring island, sheltered from the ocean by the outlying barrier island of Assateague; every year in July, Chincoteague townsfolk row over to uninhabited Assateague, round up the wild ponies that live there, make them swim across the narrow channel separating the two islands, and sell the new foals to raise money for the local fire department. *Everybody* knows that, Mom.

The good news is that you don't have to be a pony-crazed girl to enjoy a trip to Chincoteague and Assateague. Like most of this region of Maryland and Virginia, known as the Eastern Shore, it's a

Chincoteague ponies.

tranquil, wind-ruffled shore land with a lot of wildlife refuges and weather-beaten charm. You can drive right onto Chincoteague Island, home to an old fishing village that was settled by the English in the late 1600s, and from there take another causeway to Assateague, which was settled by wild horses at about the same time. Legend has it that the ponies' ancestors swam ashore from a shipwrecked Spanish galleon, but more likely they were put there by the English settlers as a natural corral. Go early in the day, because there's a quota for how many cars can be on Assateague at one time. You'll have to wait until 3pm to be allowed to drive onto the paved 4½-mile **Wildlife Drive,** which runs through the marshes and is the best place to see these shaggy, sturdy little horses. (Earlier in the day, you can walk or bicycle around this flat, easy loop to your heart's content; narrated bus tours run all day.) Besides the ponies, there are an amazing number of birds to spot, and at the end of the main road lies a splendid unspoiled beach—the **Assateague Island National Seashore**—which has bathhouses and lifeguards and a visitor center. If you're into shell collecting, the southern spit of land called Tom's Cove yields pails full.

Back in Chincoteague, there's one more must-do for pony lovers: taking a ride at the **Chincoteague Pony Centre,** 6417 Carriage Dr. (📞 **757/336-2776;** http://chincoteague.com/ponycentre/pony). Who knows—the pony you ride might be one of Misty's many descendants!

ⓘ **Chincoteague National Wildlife Refuge** (📞 757/336-6122; www.fws.gov/northeast/chinco). **Assateague Island National Seashore** (📞 410/641-1441; www.nps.gov/asis).

✈ Salisbury–Ocean City Wicomico Regional, MD, 48 miles. Norfolk International, VA, 83 miles.

🛏 $$$ **Island Motor Inn Resort,** 4391 Main St., Chincoteague (📞 **757/336-3141;** www.islandmotorinn.com). $$ **Refuge Inn,** 7058 Maddox Blvd., Chincoteague (📞 **888/257-0038** or 757/336-5511; www.refugeinn.com).

WHY THEY'LL THANK YOU: Wild horses couldn't drag us away.

In the Wild

23

El Yunque
Puerto Rico's Rainforest Gem
All ages • Rio Grande, Puerto Rico

MY CHILDREN HAVE BEEN SAVING THE RAINFOREST FOR YEARS——WHAT American child hasn't been pelted with this eco-message?—but they had never actually seen one. So they willingly gave up another day at the beach in San Juan to drive west of town to the **El Yunque National Forest.** Within seconds of stepping through its gate, we were enveloped in a lushness so profound, we knew at once that all those school recycling projects had been worth it.

Formerly known as the Caribbean National Forest, El Yunque is the only tropical rainforest in the U.S. National Forest system, a

Fantastic Aquariums & Zoos

Aquariums and zoos are a wonderful place for kids to learn, and many provide educational opportunities for young visitors. Although learning is the aim, kids will also take away the memory of coming nose to nose with a toothy shark, a giant giraffe, or some fanciful creature that will delight and awe. It's always good to bring a camera; you never know when a priceless moment of discovery may occur.

㉔ Monterey Bay Aquarium, Monterey Yes, it's huge, with more than 350,000 marine animals and plants on display, and it has two truly awesome big tanks—the million-gallon **Open Sea** exhibit, populated by yellowfin tuna, large green sea turtles, barracuda, sharks, giant ocean sunfish, and schools of bonito; and the three-story **Kelp Forest** with its stunning view of leopard sharks and other sea creatures. But what is truly striking is how this facility's displays highlight the sheer beauty of sea creatures—the feathery flutter of jellyfish, the supple grace of rays, the quicksilver flash of anchovies, sardines, and mackerel swimming in massive schools. *886 Cannery Row.* ☏ *831/648-4800; www. montereybayaquarium.org.*

㉕ The San Diego Zoo, California For most people, the highlight of this zoo is seeing the **giant pandas,** but it's also known for its vast array of species, including such rarities as the **Buerger's tree kangaroos** of New Guinea, **long billed kiwis** from New Zealand, **Przewalski's horses** from Mongolia, **lowland gorillas** from Africa, and **giant tortoises** from the Galapagos, all in naturalistic settings. In fact, the San Diego Zoo is the first zoo in the U.S. to separate animals from humans with moats instead of bars and has long been active in conservation efforts around the world as well as breeding programs for endangered species, including those beguiling black and white bears. The habitats allow the animals to feel comfortable as well as affording some great close-up views for visitors. *2920 Zoo Dr.* © *619/231-1515.* www. sandiegozoo.org.

㉖ The Bronx Zoo, New York   The Big Kahuna of New York City's wildlife parks, the 265-acre Bronx Zoo is home to more than 4,000 animals, from **Siberian tigers** and **snow lions** to its star attractions living in the **Congo Gorilla Forest** and the **Butterfly Garden**—both of them fascinating. On a good day, you can practically go nose-to-nose with one of our simian cousins through a large glass window. As befits its status as flagship zoo of the Wildlife Conservation Society, the exhibits are extremely humane, outdoors if possible, in large environments recreating the species' native habitats. This does mean that there are often long walks between exhibits, but strollers are available. As you'd expect from this New York City star, the Bronx park has lots of show-biz dazzle, with cleverly designed exhibits and novel ways of getting around. Don't miss the narrated **Wild Asia** monorail, which somehow convinces children that they've taken a 20-minute trip to the wilds of West Asia. See Brooklyn Bridge ⓴, Statue of Liberty & Ellis Island ㊶, and Metropolitan Museum of Art ㊱. *2300 Southern Blvd.* © *718/220-5100;* www.bronxzoo.com.

28,000-acre patch of virgin forest that looks pretty much the way it did when Columbus first sighted Puerto Rico back in 1493. We spent a good hour first in the **El Portal Rain Forest Center,** with its three pavilions setting forth the four separate forest microclimates that comprise the park. The best exhibit of all, though, was simply the bridge leading to the center, set high up near the tree canopy, where we got our first close-up views of the forest's lively birds. At last we hit the walking trails through the forest, and by now we knew what to look for on our hike to the waterfalls, and what to listen for—the

El Yunque National Forest.

distinctive coquí peep of the tiny tree frogs that live here in the millions. We could spot orchids blooming in the treetops, and incredibly tall ferns swaying among the tree trunks. We hiked along the quiet signposted trail to **La Mina Falls,** which announced itself through the trees as we drew closer, not only by the roar of tumbling water but also by the unmistakable salsa beat of picnicking families with portable sound systems. On this weekend day, every family in the park, it seemed, was at the falls, sitting waist-deep in deliciously cold water on the slippery, pot-holed rock shelf below the cascades.

The other trail in the park is longer and steeper: the **El Yunque trail,** which winds upward through forests of sierra palm and palo colorado, before descending into the dwarf forest of **Mount Britton,** which is often shrouded in clouds. There are great views here from various peaks, including **Yunque Rock.**

The weather looked overcast when we started out, and at one point a light rain shower began to spatter upon the canopy, barely enough to get us wet. Somehow, that seemed absolutely perfect. After all, what should you expect in a rainforest if not rain?

(i) **El Yunque National Forest,** PR 191 (© **787/888-1880;** www.
fs.fed.us/r8/caribbean).

✈ Luis Muñoz Marín International, San Juan, 40km (25 miles).

🛏 $$ **Comfort Inn,** Calle Clemenceau 6, San Juan (© **800/858-
7407** or 787/721-0170; www.comfortinn.com). $$ **The Gallery
Inn,** Calle Norzagaray 204–206, Old San Juan (© **866/572-2783** or
787/722-1808; www.thegalleryinn.com).

WHY THEY'LL THANK YOU: Hearing the coquís.

27 Fossils

Dinosaur Valley
In the Tracks of the Dinosaurs
All ages • Glen Rose, Texas

EVEN THE VERY YOUNGEST DINOSAUR LOVERS—AND AREN'T PRESCHOOL-
ers the biggest dinosaur fans there are?—can interpret the fossil
record left in stone at Dinosaur Valley: The huge footprints in the
rocks here are so unmistakable, it's easy to picture the prehistoric
theropods and sauropods who made them 110 million years ago.

You'll find the prints beside the Paluxy River, a branch of the
Brazos, which winds through this shady, lovely 1,500-acre park in
Texas, about an hour's drive southwest of Fort Worth. Late summer, when the river is low, is the best time to come. You can dis-
cern the footprints best when the rock is just slightly underwater,
with the wetness darkening it. (Bring a whisk broom with you to
clear any debris.) It's strikingly evident that two different types of
dinosaurs walked in the moist limy mud that formed this rock.
Many of the footprints (typically 15–25 in. long) show three toes
and sharp claws, indicating a meat-eating dinosaur called *Acrocanthosaurus.* This guy stood 20 to 30 feet tall and walked on two legs.
The even larger footprints (some more than 3¼ ft. long) were made
by long-necked plant-eating dinosaurs, your basic sauropods (nicknamed **"brontosaurs"**). The kids can tell its front tracks from its

back ones: The front feet were round with peglike toes, like elephants' feet, while the back ones had large claws angling rearward. Most likely these were left by a 30- to 50-foot-long dinosaur named *Pleurocoelus*.

The tracks can easily be seen at two spots in the park: The main site is across the northwest parking lot and down some stone steps to the river; upstream is the Blue Hole, a sinkhole with many more brontosaur tracks (it's also a great place for swimming, so bring your suits). The kids will have no trouble imagining a scenario of the carnivorous Acrocanthosaurus stalking the gentle, slow-moving Pleurocoelus (originally a slab of tracks showed the meat-eater ambushing the plant-eater—to see that slab today, unfortunately, you'd need to be in New York City at the American Museum of Natural History). But what's still here is graphic evidence indeed.

The visitor center has replicas, foot skeletons, murals, and diagrams to help kids visualize the dinosaurs. What's more, outdoors stand two immense fiberglass models, one of a brown T-Rex and the other of a green Apatosaurus—relics of the Dinosaur World exhibit at the 1964 New York World's Fair. Built by the Sinclair Oil Company (remember the old Sinclair gas station sign with its green brontosaurus?), these models are historic artifacts in their own right. Scientists still argue over what the head of the Apatosaurus should look like, but hey, we're all still learning.

(i) (C) **254/897-4588;** www.tpwd.state.tx.us/spdest/findadest/parks/dinosaur_valley.

✈ Dallas–Fort Worth International, 75 miles.

🛏 $ **Residence Inn Fort Worth University,** 1701 S. University Dr., Ft. Worth (C **888/236-2427** or 817/870-1011; www.marriott.com/hotels/travel/dfwrp). $$$ **Stockyards Hotel,** 109 E. Exchange Ave., Ft. Worth (C **800/423-8471** or 817/625-6427; www.stockyardshotel.com).

WHY THEY'LL THANK YOU: Dinosaurs walked here.

La Brea Tar Pits
Oozing Ancient History
Ages 6 & up • Los Angeles, California

AN ODOROUS SWAMP OF GOOEY ASPHALT OOZES TO THE EARTH'S surface in the middle of Los Angeles. No, it's not a low-budget horror-movie set—it's the La Brea Tar Pits, a bizarre primal pool on Museum Row where hot tar has been seeping to the surface from a subterranean oil field for more than 40,000 years. It's an incongruous sight in the middle of built-up Los Angeles; in this grassy patch of Hancock Park, you can walk right up to the abandoned asphalt quarry's slick black pool of oily water, inhaling its acrid scent and watching bubbles of methane gas bloop to the steamy surface. Suddenly the high-rise office towers of Wilshire and Fairfax boulevards seem to recede, and you can imagine a distant past when mammoths and saber-tooth cats prowled this fern-shaded landscape.

The **bubbling pools** have tempted thirsty animals throughout history—with fatal consequences. Nearly 400 species of mammals, birds, amphibians, and fish, many of them now extinct, walked, crawled, landed, swam, or slithered into the sticky sludge, got stuck in the worst way, and stayed forever. For many years, their fossilized bones were pried out of hardened asphalt by the pit's owners, who were too busy extracting commercial tar to care about them. But, because paleontology came of age in the early 20th century, in 1906, scientists began to study this prehistoric trove. Some 100 tons of **fossils** were eventually removed—ground sloths, giant vultures, mastodons, camels, bears, native lions, dire wolves, lizards, and relatives of today's super-rats—the world's largest collection of Ice Age remains.

Today those entombed specimens are displayed at the adjacent **Page Museum.** Some 30 complete skeletons, along with assorted skulls and other bones, are handsomely mounted with in-depth explanations; there are also a few animatronic figures flailing about, though nothing that would terrify young children. Advise them not to expect dinosaurs—these fossils are all from the Ice Age, but in fact those are even rarer than dinosaur fossils. Until we came here, I never knew that there were native horses in prehistoric North America (they became extinct long before the conquistadors arrived with their European horses). Archaeological work is ongoing; you can watch as scientists clean, identify, and catalog new finds in the Paleontology Laboratory.

This quarry has always been open to the public, and thankfully it hasn't been walled off and overcommercialized (the kitschy figures of struggling mastodons set outdoor in the pits are time-warp quaint). Poking around the park, I felt as much connected to the 1950s, when I first visited California, as I did to the Ice Age. Somehow in all my trips to L.A., I had never before made time for the La Brea Tar Pits. And now, at last, I was here, and it was so much cooler than the glitzy theme parks and Hollywood Boulevard attractions. I was thankful to be able to introduce it to my kids.

ⓘ 5801 Wilshire Blvd. (📞 **323/934-PAGE** [7243]; www.tarpits. org).

✈ Los Angeles International.

🛏 $$$ **The Beverly Garland Holiday Inn,** 4222 Vineland Ave., North Hollywood (📞 **800/BEVERLY** [238-3759] or 818/980-8000; www.beverlygarland.com). $$ **Hollywood Roosevelt Hotel,** 7000 Hollywood Blvd. (📞 **800/950-7667** or 323/466-7000; www. hollywoodroosevelt.com).

WHY THEY'LL THANK YOU: Mastodons checked in, but they never checked out.

Cahokia Mounds

Metropolis of the Ancient Mississippians

Ages 6 & up • Collinsville, Illinois

IT WAS ONCE THE BIGGEST CITY NORTH OF MEXICO, WITH SOMEWHERE around 20,000 residents—farmers, hunters, craftsmen, traders, priests—at its peak in A.D. 1100–1200. Archaeologists have named them the Mississippians, but we don't know what they called themselves, because they left no writings behind. An air of mystery hangs over this site, just across the Mississippi River from St. Louis. Who were these people and what was their world like? The answers are hauntingly elusive.

Exhibits at the site's visitor center show how archaeologists play detective with the ancient past. The variety of arrowheads dug up, for example, proves that these people were sophisticated enough to trade with tribes as far away as southern Minnesota and the Gulf Coast. Experts gather that the mounds were built by hand, with workers carrying dirt in baskets on their backs from so-called "borrow pits" to the mounds. Ordinary citizens apparently lived in simple houses with pole walls and thatched roofs, but they labored to erect these immense earthen structures—109 still exist, 68 of them in this park—for public ceremonies.

After viewing the center's model of the ancient city, you can take tours of three different sections of the 2,200-acre site—hour-long ranger-led tours, or 30- to 45-minute self-guided walks (maps and audiotapes available; iPod tours are also offered for a fee) of each area. You certainly can't miss **Monks Mound,** a four-terraced platform mound that once held the home of the city's ruler; it's the biggest mound in the western hemisphere, covering 16 acres at its base and rising 100 feet. Climb the modern steps to its now-grass-covered flat top, and you gaze over a huge leveled plaza, bounded by the city's 2-mile-long log stockade wall, bits of which have been reconstructed. From this vantage point, the kids can identify several mound shapes—flat-top, conical, ridge-top—which apparently had various purposes. Unlike other cultures, the Mississippians generally did not use mounds for burials, although in a few cases skeletons have been unearthed with all the trappings of a prince or chieftain; other skeletons found are mostly those of young women or men with hands and feet cut off, which suggests they were human sacrifices. (Mound 72 was particularly full of sacrificial burials.)

Once archaeologists started to dig, they found something even more amazing: the remains of an astronomical observatory, similar to Stonehenge but built of red cedar logs instead of stones: **Woodhenge,** the scientists have named it. How did two prehistoric cultures on different continents each get the same idea? And why did this great Mississippian city die? Archaeologists keep on digging, for they still have a lot of questions to answer.

(ⓘ) 30 Ramey St. (🕾 **618/346-5160;** www.cahokiamounds.com).

✈ Lambert–St. Louis International, St. Louis, MO, 22 miles.

🛏 $$ **Drury Inn Union Station,** 201 S. 20th St., St. Louis, MO (🕾 **800/378-7946** or 314/231-3900; www.druryhotels.com). $$$ **Embassy Suites,** 11237 Lone Eagle Dr., Bridgeton, MO (🕾 **800/362-2779** or 314/739-8929; embassysuites1.hilton.com).

WHY THEY'LL THANK YOU: Ancient mysteries, right in America's backyard.

Early Humans **30**

Canyon de Chelly
Hanging Out with the Anasazi
Ages 8 & up • Chinle, Arizona

FOR NEARLY 5,000 YEARS, PEOPLE HAVE MADE THEIR HOMES IN THIS spectacular pair of narrow sandstone canyons of remote northeastern Arizona. The Navajos are the most recent guardians of this

Navajo ruins in Canyon de Chelly.

land; the Ancestral Puebloans (also known as the Anasazi) left their mark too, in the giant rock amphitheaters where they created caves, dwelling rooms, and ceremonial kivas. To explore the canyons is to see centuries unfold.

Ancestral Puebloan civilization reached its zenith between A.D. 1100 and 1300, but evidence suggests that these canyons may have been occupied as early as A.D. 300. In the nooks and crannies of the canyons, you'll see ancient dwellings hollowed into the rock walls and the circular sacred rooms known as kivas; the largest and most impressive ruin is the **White House Ruin** in Canyon de Chelly, which was inhabited between 1040 and 1275. You'll also see ancient tombs—the **Tomb of the Weaver** near the **Antelope House Ruin,** and the **Mummy Caves,** both appropriately enough in **Canyon del Muerto,** or the Canyon of the Dead.

While most tourists simply drive along the two scenic drives— the 15-mile North Rim Drive, which overlooks Canyon del Muerto, and the 16-mile South Rim Drive, which overlooks Canyon de Chelly (pronounced "duh shay")—hire a guide and you can take the kids right down into the canyons, where they can poke around these fascinating ruins. Navajo guides or local tour companies will lead you either on foot or in a four-wheel-drive vehicle. The hike down is fairly demanding, so with kids you'll probably opt to drive—there'll still be a bit of walking to reach the various ruins.

Because you'll be seeing both Navajo and Ancestral Puebloan relics, make sure the kids learn the difference between the two kinds of rock art. Look for dark slick streaks on the canyon walls, created by water seepage reacting with iron oxide—ancestral Puebloans chipped away at this so-called "desert varnish" to expose the lighter-colored rock underneath, forming pictorial designs we now call petroglyphs. Pictographs are similar designs made later by the Navajos, applying colorful paints directly to the sandstone walls to commemorate important tribal events. Urge the kids to take time to decipher the stories told by the rock pictures—they're windows into an ancient way of life.

ⓘ Off U.S. 191 (℃ **928/674-5500**; www.nps.gov/cach).

✈ Flagstaff Pulliam, 222 miles.

🛏 $$ **Holiday Inn Canyon de Chelly,** Indian Rte. 7 (𝒞 **888/ HOLIDAY** [465-4329] or 928/674-5000; www.ichotelsgroup.com).
$$ **Thunderbird Lodge,** Indian Rte. 7 (𝒞 **800/679-2473** or 928/ 674-5841; www.tbirdlodge.com).

WHY THEY'LL THANK YOU: Seeing pictographs and petroglyphs.

31 Early Humans

Puako Petroglyphs
Hawaiian History Carved in Stone
Ages 6 & up • Big Island, Hawaii

IN THE ANCIENT HAWAIIAN LANGUAGE, THEY CALL IT "MANA"—THE spiritual force that flows through all creation. Some places in the Hawaiian Islands have a particularly powerful mana, and this was one of them: A shelf of pahoehoe lava rock the size of a football field, hidden in a tangle of forest on the Kohala Coast, overlooking the vast Pacific, where early Hawaiian artists carved a panoply of arresting figures, some 3,000 strong.

In the complicated history of modern Hawaii, all too often native Hawaiian culture was obliterated by white European settlers, but not this time. The developers of the Mauna Lani resort, setting out to design a new golf course for its Orchid hotel, discovered this amazing site in the scrubby woods and respectfully set it aside in its own protected park. It takes about half an hour to hike the winding trail through the tough little trees that sprang up on this hardened lava flow, but when we made that last turn and saw the great sheet of dark jagged rock, etched over and over with a joyous riot of figures . . . I swear my son and I felt the mana wash over us.

These petroglyphs served many functions: as historical record, as a repository of sacred legend, and as beautiful art. The skilled artists who carved these figures followed a strict, highly stylized iconography (don't skip the plaques at the beginning of the trail, where a series of reproduction stones display the significant symbols; kids can make rubbings here). Once you've reached the real petroglyphs, you won't be allowed to walk on the fragile lava rock, but circle around the railing and pick out individual figures: dancers and paddlers, fishermen and chiefs, hundreds of marchers all in a row, and many family groups, probably honoring specific clans. Images from daily life crop up everywhere: fish hooks, spears, poi pounders, outrigger canoes. The best way to see it is on a guided walk, available from the Fairmont Orchid concierge; the guide will point out special figures, including some kites (proof of ancient contact with the Maoris in New Zealand) and the first of the sailing ships that heralded a new era for the islands. Bonus points for whoever can find the single snake in the whole tableau. Come early or late in the day, when the sun's slanting rays hit the carvings in sharp relief.

The **Puako Petroglyphs** are the island's most spectacular—in fact, this is the largest rock art site in the entire Pacific—but there are several others along this coast, the sacred domain of Hawaii's ancient kings. At the **Waikoloa Beach Resort,** off Hwy. 19 just south of the Mauna Lani, free tours of the property's petroglyphs leave from the Kings' Shops (Thurs–Sun 10:30am; *©* **808/886-8811**). Farther south along Hwy. 19, the **Kona Village Resort** (*©* **800/ 367-5290** or 808/325-5555; www.konavillage.com) is home to the Kaupulehu Petroglyphs. At press time, Kona Village was closed due to damage caused by the March 2011 tsunami; call ahead to see whether it's started offering petroglyph tours again. You may also want to head for the other end of the Mauna Lani property, to see the Hawaiian kings' ingenious fish farm: the **Kalahuipuaa Fish Ponds,** preserved in a suitably royal tropical beachside setting.

ⓘ Holoholokai Beach Park, off Hwy. 19, in the Mauna Lani Resort, N. Kaniku Dr.

✈ Kona International.

🛏 $$$ **The Fairmont Orchid,** 1 N. Kaniku Dr. (*©* **866/540-4474** or 808/885-2000; www.fairmont.com/orchid). $ **Kona Tiki Hotel,** 75-5968 Alii Dr., Kailua-Kona (*©* **808/329-1425;** www.kona tikihotel.com).

WHY THEY'LL THANK YOU: Feel the mana.

Lexington & Concord
The Shot Heard 'Round the World
Ages 6 & up • Concord, Lexington & Lincoln, Massachusetts

THE OPENING SALVOS OF THE AMERICAN REVOLUTION—THE SO-called Shot Heard 'Round the World—were fired in the villages of Lexington and Concord, Massachusetts, on April 19, 1775. No need to memorize the date; you'll hear it everywhere when you visit **Minute Man National Historical Park.** After I read my favorite childhood book, *Johnny Tremain,* to my kids, we just had to come here to see where the climactic battle really happened—and they loved it.

To take things in chronological order, begin in Lexington, where two messengers from Boston, Paul Revere and William Dawes, raised the alarm late on the night of April 18. The **visitor center** on the town common—or Battle Green, as they call it—has a diorama of the early-morning skirmish between local militia, known as "Minutemen" for their ability to assemble quickly, and a large force of British troops. The statue on the green depicts Capt. John Parker, who commanded the militia. At the **Hancock-Clarke House,** 36 Hancock St., patriot leaders

Minuteman statue in Lexington, Massachusetts.

55

John Hancock and Samuel Adams were awakened by Revere and Dawes. You can also tour **Buckman Tavern,** 1 Bedford St. (© **781/862-1703**), on the green, where the Minutemen assembled at dawn. (Both historic houses are closed during the off season, so call ahead for hours and dates of operation if you're hoping to go inside.) Ordered to disperse, the ragtag (and no doubt sleepy) band of colonists stood their ground—fewer than 100 poorly armed colonists versus some 700 red-coated British soldiers. Nobody knows who started the shooting, but when it was over, 8 militia members lay dead, including a drummer boy, and 10 were wounded.

Next move on to Concord, where the British proceeded in search of stockpiled arms (which militia members had already moved). Begin at the **North Bridge Visitor Center,** 174 Liberty St., with its diorama and video program, and then proceed down Monument Street to the **Minute Man National Historical Park** (© **978/369-6993;** www.nps.gov/mima). A path leads from the parking lot to the one don't-miss sight, **North Bridge,** where a much larger force of Minutemen massed to attack British regulars and set off the war's first full-fledged battle. Narrative plaques and audio presentations along the path describe the onset of the battle; Daniel Chester French's famous Minuteman statue stands nobly poised by the bridge.

Drive east on Lexington Road to the next park section, where you can follow the **Battle Road Trail,** a 5.5-mile interpretive path (wheelchair, stroller, and bicycle accessible) tracing the route of the defeated British troops straggling back toward Boston. (In summer, ask at the visitor centers about ranger-led guided tours along Battle Rd.) Near the eastern entrance of the park, the **Minute Man Visitor Center,** 250 N. Great Rd., Lincoln (off Rte. 2A), has a fascinating multimedia program about the Revolution and a 40-foot mural illustrating the battle.

ⓘ**Lexington Visitors Center,** 1875 Massachusetts Ave., Lexington (© **781/862-1450;** www.lexingtonchamber.org), or **Lexington Historical Society** (© **781/862-1703;** www.lexingtonhistory.org). **Concord Visitor Center,** 58 Main St., Concord (© **978/369-3120;** www.concordchamberofcommerce.org).

✈ Boston Logan International, 18 miles.

🛏 $$ **DoubleTree Suites by Hilton,** 400 Soldiers Field Rd.
(📞 **800/222-TREE** [8733] or 617/783-0090; www.doubletree.com).
$ **The Midtown Hotel,** 220 Huntington Ave. (📞 **800/343-1177** or
617/262-1000; www.midtownhotel.com).

WHY THEY'LL THANK YOU: Listen my children, and you shall
hear . . .

33 Battle Sites

Remembering the Alamo

Ages 4 & up • San Antonio, Texas

VISITING SAN ANTONIO WITHOUT GOING TO THE ALAMO IS LIKE VISIT-
ing London and not seeing Big Ben: You can do it, but it would be
wrong.

Expect the kids to be let down at first. The Alamo looks down-
right dinky, set smack in the heart of downtown San Antonio, sur-
rounded by skyscrapers and traffic. But the whole point of the
Alamo is that it *was* such a tiny fort, and the valiant Texan volun-
teers never had a ghost of a chance of escaping the Mexican
army's siege—and still they fought, they fought to the death.
That's heroism, Texas style.

There were only 188 Texans defending the Alamo in February
1836, facing the 4,000-strong army of General Santa Anna, who
was bent on squashing the Texas territory's bid for independence
from the new Mexican Republic. The Texans held out doggedly for
13 days, waiting for reinforcements that never arrived, until all the
men—every last one of them, including pioneer heroes Davy
Crockett and Jim Bowie—were killed in a crushing dawn attack on
March 6. But a month later, when Sam Houston was leading
another troop of Texans into the battle of San Jacinto, he fired
them up with the cry, "Remember the Alamo!" With that heroic
example to live up to, the Texans fought like demons, and this time
they won, becoming the independent Republic of Texas. (It didn't
join the U.S. until 1846.)

What you see today isn't much of a fort—in 1836 the fortified compound was a bit larger, its outer walls ringing much of what is today Alamo Plaza (look for foundation stones near the steps down to River Walk). After the defeat at San Jacinto, the retreating Mexican forces pulled down much of the Alamo fort to prevent the Texans from refortifying it. Only two original buildings remain. First is the gabled stone **mission church**—now officially a shrine, so show respect by removing hats and taking no photos—which was built in 1756 for the Mission San Antonio de Valero, founded in 1718 to convert local Native American tribes. By the end of the 18th century, the mission was turned over to a Spanish cavalry unit, which renamed it the Alamo (Spanish for "cottonwood") after their Mexican hometown. Besides the church, you can visit the **Long Barracks,** originally the missionaries' living quarters and later used as the cavalry's barracks; today it includes exhibits on **Texas history,** with an emphasis on the Alamo battle.

For kids, however, it's the **artifacts** displayed in the church that will be most compelling: things like a Bowie knife, Crockett's buckskin jacket, and one of the antiquated flintlock rifles the Texans used to defend the fort. Several cannons from the battle are set around the courtyard, mute witnesses to that day of incredible valor.

ⓘ 300 Alamo Plaza (✆ **210/225-1391;** www.thealamo.org).

✈ San Antonio International, 13 miles.

🛏 $$ **Crockett Hotel,** 320 Bonham St. (✆ **800/292-1050** or 210/225-6500; www.crocketthotel.com).

WHY THEY'LL THANK YOU: Heroes against all odds.

Gettysburg National Park
Blood & Sorrow in the Civil War

Ages 6 & up • Gettysburg, Pennsylvania

"AWESOME" DOESN'T BEGIN TO DO JUSTICE TO THIS VAST BATTLE-ground, where thousands of Union and Confederate soldiers clashed for 3 sultry July days in 1863. As Abraham Lincoln himself said in his famous 1864 speech here, this land has been conse-crated by blood—over 50,000 deaths—and an almost-eerie atmo-sphere hangs over this tranquil patch of rolling farmland, now peppered with war monuments.

The park visitor center has several excellent exhibits that will help you get oriented—after all, the battle raged over a large patch of country in the course of 3 days, and there's a lot to keep straight. Don't miss the historic *Battle of Gettysburg* **cyclorama painting,** an incredibly detailed 360-degree depiction of Pickett's Charge which was painted in 1883—it's just the sort of pre-video-era spe-cial effect I love. At the tour desk, you can buy CDs for self-guided driving tours around the 250-acre battle site, but we found that this was one place where it paid to invest in a personal guide, who drove us in our station wagon around the battlefield for 2 hours (reserve at least 3 days in advance). Gettysburg's guides are gold mines of Civil War information, tailoring the tour to your particular interests; there wasn't a question we lobbed at him that he couldn't handle, whether biographies of the commanders or the physics of cannon fusillades.

We were completely engrossed by **Seminary Ridge,** where the main Confederate forces were camped; we could look down the hillside where the heroes of Pickett's Charge plunged to their gal-lant end. But we were most moved by **Little Round Top,** where a plucky band of Northern soldiers held the high ground against a furious Confederate onslaught surging up out of the boulder-strewn hollow called Devil's Den. Observation towers near Semi-nary Ridge give you a great aerial overview, but walking around the

Cannons in Gettysburg National Park.

landscape is the only way to appreciate how hard-won every inch of ground was.

In the town of Gettysburg itself, we enjoyed the **American Civil War Museum,** 297 Steinwehr Ave. (© **717/334-6245;** www. gettysburgmuseum.com), which tells the full Civil War history in waxwork dioramas; normally I find wax figures hokey or creepy but this was actually tasteful and informative. The most special part of our visit, though, was seeing the costumed re-enactors—many of them amateur Civil War buffs here for the fun of it—roaming around the town and the park, socializing around campfires or demonstrating their rifle skills. For a flicker of a moment we traveled through time, feeling the Gettysburg tragedy in our bones.

ⓘ **Visitor Center,** 1195 Baltimore Pike (© **717/334-1124;** www. nps.gov/gett). **Advance tickets,** call © **877/874-2478** or 717/334-2436 (www.gettysburgfoundation.org).

✈ Harrisburg International, Middletown, PA, 35 miles. Baltimore/ Washington International Thurgood Marshall, Baltimore, MD, 60 miles.

☐ $$$ **1863 Inn of Gettysburg,** 516 Baltimore St. (© **866/953-4483** or 717/334-6211; www.1863innofgettysburg.com). $$ **Quality Inn Gettysburg Motor Lodge,** 380 Steinwehr Ave. (© **800/228-5151** or 717/334-1103; www.gettysburgqualityinn.com).

WHY THEY'LL THANK YOU: Brother fought brother on this bloody ground.

---

35 **WWII & the Cold War**

Pearl Harbor
Day of Infamy
Ages 8 & up • Honolulu, Hawaii

TODAY HAWAII IS SO SYNONYMOUS WITH LEIS, LUAUS, AND TROPICAL suntans, it's weird to realize that most Americans had barely heard of this South Pacific U.S. possession before December 7, 1941, when the horrifying news came over the radio: Japanese bombers had attacked U.S. ships at Pearl Harbor, Honolulu. Hawaii wasn't even a state, but it was still American soil, which was under attack for the first time since the War of 1812. President Franklin D. Roosevelt called it "a date which will live in infamy"; after years of pretending that World War II wasn't our fight, we realized it was.

Pearl Harbor is a site that inspires reflection on war and peace and our place in the global community. The **USS *Arizona* Memorial** at Pearl Harbor is a truly special monument. Just 6 feet below the surface of the sea, you can see the deck of the 608-foot battleship USS *Arizona,* which sank in a swift 9 minutes, killing 1,177 of its men, more than half the total casualties that tragic day. Oil still oozes up from its engine room to stain the harbor's calm blue water—some say the ship's still weeping for its lost crew. Moored a short distance from shore, the memorial is a stark white rectangle with a scooped-out roof that spans the hull of the ruined ship; on its walkways you can ponder over the ship's bell, dredged up from the wreckage, and a shrine room with the inscribed names of the

The USS *Arizona* Memorial at Pearl Harbor.

dead. The gallant flagpole overhead is attached to the mainmast of the sunken ship. You'll ride out to the memorial on Navy launches from the visitor center; go early if you can, because you'll wait 2 to 3 hours at midday. A 20-minute film and exhibits at the center fill in the history for the kids while you're waiting for your assigned ship time.

Two other ships in the harbor tell the rest of the World War II story, so you're not left on a tragic note. Next to the Arizona, you can board a World War II submarine, the **USS Bowfin** (© 808/423-1341; www.bowfin.org), nicknamed the "Pearl Harbor Avenger" for the way it harried the Japanese throughout the rest of the war. This is a great place to see how submariners lived in their cramped underwater quarters. From the Bowfin's visitor center you can also visit the **USS Missouri** (© 877/MIGHTYMO [644-4896] or 808/455-1600; www.ussmissouri.com), a 58,000-ton battleship that fought at Tokyo, Iwo Jima, and Okinawa. Fittingly, the Japanese surrender was signed on September 2, 1945, on the deck of the *Missouri*. The guided tour, complete with 1940s music played on the shuttles to the ship, is a fascinating look at a massive seagoing vessel.

(i) Pearl Harbor ((c) **808/422-3300**; www.nps.gov/usar).

✈ Honolulu International.

🛏 $$$ **Outrigger Waikiki on the Beach,** 2335 Kalakaua Ave. ((c) **866/956-4262** or 808/923-0711; www.outrigger.com). $ **Kai Aloha Apartment Hotel,** 235 Saratoga Rd. ((c) **808/923-6723;** www.kaialohahotel.com).

WHY THEY'LL THANK YOU: Seeing history with their own eyes.

---

36 | **WWII & the Cold War**

The International Spy Museum
Combat under Cover
Ages 6 & up • Washington, D.C.

LEAVING BEHIND ALL OF D.C.'S WORTHY MALL MUSEUMS AND SNEAKing up to F Street to see the Spy Museum seemed like a guilty pleasure. But the parents in our group all grew up in the era of *Goldfinger, I Spy,* and *The Man From U.N.C.L.E.,* and we were hot to see it, however schlocky. The kids trailed along, expecting some sort of *Get Smart*–ish romp. But what impressed me most was that this smartly packaged attraction is also plenty educational—a little science here, a little history there, lots of geography—so we didn't have to feel guilty at all.

The entryway to the museum has a certain clandestine allure, as you pass through a blue-neon-lit tunnel and step into a very secure-looking elevator. We could have stayed forever in the **School for Spies** section, devoted to the tradecraft of espionage—everything from buttonhole cameras and invisible ink to microdots and disguised weapons. Several interactive kiosks let the kids hone their own skills, from detecting the bugging devices in a room to spotting covert activity in a seemingly harmless videoed street scene. The movie connection runs strong here, with a gadget-laden Bond car and a display of disguise techniques developed by Hollywood makeup artists. The kids were visibly getting drawn in.

The next gallery traces **intelligence gathering** through the ages, proving that the modern age has no monopoly on paranoia and secrecy—even leaders such as Moses and George Washington used secret agents, and don't get me started on the spying that went on in Tudor England (that's how Sir Walter Raleigh ended up in the Tower of London). I hadn't before thought of the Underground Railroad as a spy network, but what else was it, with all its secret codes and furtive activity?

The **World War II** section was especially gripping, partly because so many artifacts still exist (all declassified now, evidently). Hindsight is 20/20, they say, but it was shocking to learn how the U.S. government ignored spy warnings of Japan's imminent attack on Pearl Harbor (reminiscent of the unheeded FBI warnings before 9/11), and how the super-secret technology behind the first atom bomb slipped into the wrong hands. The section on **Bletchley Park,** where British code breakers feverishly worked to break Germany's famed Enigma code, engrossed me so much, the kids literally had to pull me away. Then we turned a corner and the **Cold War** was upon us, the great face-off between the CIA and the KGB that made paranoids of all us baby boomers. I loved this section, especially the reconstruction of an East Berlin street corner, on top of the CIA's high-tech surveillance tunnel beneath the Soviet Embassy. Classic John le Carré territory.

Coming out 2 hours later, the kids peppered us with questions: What was the Cold War all about, and who was this Cardinal Richelieu, and was the guy who wrote *Chitty Chitty Bang Bang* really a spy? Forget the PlayStation they were longing to get back to. . . .

ⓘ 800 F St. NW (📞 **202/393-7798;** www.spymuseum.org).

✈ Ronald Reagan Washington National, 5 miles. Washington Dulles International, 26 miles. Baltimore/Washington International Thurgood Marshall, 30 miles.

🛏 $$ **Embassy Suites,** 1250 22nd St. NW (📞 **800/EMBASSY** [362-2779] or 202/857-3388; www.embassysuites.com). $$ **Georgetown Suites,** 1000 29th St. NW & 1111 30th St. NW, Georgetown (📞 **800/348-7203** or 202/298-7800; www.georgetownsuites.com).

WHY THEY'LL THANK YOU: Being Bond for an afternoon.

San Juan Fortress
New World Outpost
All ages • San Juan, Puerto Rico

As USUAL, WE WERE FEELING ANTSY 2 DAYS INTO OUR BEACH vacation, yearning for some proper sightseeing. As we drove through Old San Juan, the Caribbean's biggest historic district, the boys leaned eagerly out the taxi windows, wondering what lay at the end of those thick city walls barricading the Atlantic seacoast. Then we came to the end of Calle Norzagaray and saw it: El Morro, the staunch old fort commanding the rocky point at the entrance to San Juan Bay. A sweep of smooth green lawn (perfect for kite flying) sets it apart from the historic town it was built to protect; beyond the ramparts lies one of the most dramatic views in the Caribbean. Now *there* is a *fort*.

El Morro (the name means "headland") was built by Spanish colonists in 1539, long before any English settlers showed up in North America. Of course, it wasn't this big at first: Originally it was just one stout round tower, now encased in the seaward core of the fort. More walls and cannon-firing positions were added over the years, until by 1787 the citadel had filled out to the current plan, an intriguing labyrinth of dungeons, barracks, vaults, lookouts, iron grates, and bulwarks. Over the main entrance, as you cross a bridge over a dry grassed-in moat, notice the Spanish royal coat of arms carved in stone. The upper plaza, where soldiers drilled and officers were quartered, faces the city to defend the fort from land; go down a long, steep ramp, designed for moving wheeled cannons, to the lower plaza and you're facing out to sea. (The enlisted men lived here, in cramped barracks.) Starting with an attack from Sir Francis Drake in 1595, this Spanish stronghold withstood many onslaughts over the centuries from both the English and the Dutch. The United States bombarded it in 1898 during the Spanish-American War—and by the end of that war, Puerto Rico had become a U.S. possession.

Although there are historical exhibits set up around the fort, little has been done to furnish its rooms—nothing to distract from

El Morro.

the massive, impregnable battlements of sand-colored stone, and that's what my sons most remember about it. Nowadays it's run by the National Park Service as part of the **San Juan National Historic Site,** combining El Morro with **Fort San Cristóbal,** the newer (1634) and larger fort a mile to the east. The combined visitor center has a film and historic exhibits, set in a World War II strategic military base that's connected to San Cristóbal by tunnels.

ⓘ **San Juan National Historic Site,** Calle Norzagaray (𝄓 **787/ 729-6777**; www.nps.gov/saju).

✈ Luis Muñoz Marín International, San Juan.

🛏 $$ **Comfort Inn,** Calle Clemenceau 6, Condado (𝄓 **877/424- 6423** or 787/721-0170; www.comfortinn.com). $$$ **Ritz-Carlton San Juan,** Av. de los Gobernadores 6961, Isla Verde (𝄓 **800/542- 8680** or 787/253-1700; www.ritzcarlton.com).

WHY THEY'LL THANK YOU: Standing on the mighty ramparts, looking out across the blue Caribbean.

Plimoth Plantation
The Pilgrims' Progress
All ages • Plymouth, Massachusetts

EVERY AMERICAN SCHOOLCHILD KNOWS ABOUT PLYMOUTH—ABOUT how a band of English pilgrims, fleeing religious persecution, left Europe on the *Mayflower* and set up a settlement at Plymouth in December 1620. What you won't know until you visit is how small everything was, from the perilously tiny *Mayflower* to the landing point at Plymouth Rock. But rather than feel disappointed, children may be awed to realize just how difficult this venture was and how brave the settlers were to attempt what they did.

The logical place to begin (good luck talking kids out of it) is at **Plymouth Rock.** This landing place of the *Mayflower* passengers was originally 15 feet long and 3 feet wide, though it has eroded

Plimoth Plantation.

over the centuries and been moved many times. The 1920 portico that protects that much-dwindled rock makes it even harder to imagine Pilgrims springing off the boat onto shore, but thankfully the rock is complemented by the **Mayflower II**, a Plimoth Plantation attraction berthed beside Plymouth Rock. It's a full-scale replica of the type of ship that brought the Pilgrims to America in 1620; you'll be amazed that 102 voyagers survived a transatlantic voyage on a wooden vessel only 107 feet long. Costumed guides give first-person accounts of the voyage, and alongside the ship museum shops provide a stage set of early Pilgrim dwellings.

Having landed, now you're ready for the big attraction: **Plimoth Plantation,** an extensive re-creation of the 1627 Pilgrim village. Enter by the hilltop fort that protected the village and walk down to the farm area, visiting homes and gardens constructed with careful attention to historic detail. Plimoth has some of the most convincing costumed reenactors in the country, who chat with visitors while going about daily tasks as they were done in the 1600s. Sometimes you can join the activities—perhaps planting, harvesting, witnessing a trial, or visiting a wedding party. Though the Pilgrims enjoyed friendly relations with the native Wampanoags (the nearby **Wampanoag Homesite** re-creates their village), the plantation's Pilgrims still conduct daily militia drills with matchlock muskets, no doubt because boys like my sons so adore weapons demonstrations. Your ticket (buy a combination ticket with the *Mayflower II*) is good for 2 days' admission, so no need to rush through the site—there's too much to see.

A few non-Plantation sites in town are worth a stop. **Pilgrim Hall Museum,** 75 Court St. (© **508/746-1620;** www.pilgrimhall. org), displays original artifacts like Myles Standish's sword and Governor Bradford's Bible. Then visit **Burial Hill,** right off of Town Square, and **Cole's Hill,** on Carver Street, to see the graves of the Pilgrims who died that first winter—more or less half the original group, a sobering statistic indeed.

ⓘ 137 Warren Ave. (© **508/746-1622;** www.plimoth.org).

✈ Boston Logan International, 40 miles.

🛏 $$ **John Carver Inn,** 25 Summer St. (© **800/274-1620** or 508/746-7100; www.johncarverinn.com).

BEST TIME: Open late March to November.

WHY THEY'LL THANK YOU: Makes Thanksgiving more than just a turkey dinner.

39 **Forging a Nation**

Williamsburg, Jamestown & Yorktown
Virginia's Colonial Past
All ages • Virginia

ONE OF OUR BEST FAMILY VACATIONS EVER WAS A 3-DAY GETAWAY TO Colonial Williamsburg, one of those summer trips we'd postponed for years, waiting until all three kids were old enough to make sense of its history. The weather was sweltering hot, then pouring rain—and none of that mattered. Williamsburg works on so many levels, it's a slam-dunk. The kids learned a lot, but they also had more fun than we ever expected.

It's also a relative bargain, considering how much Williamsburg offers for the money. Rockefeller money underwrites the 301-acre site of Virginia's colonial capital, sprucely maintaining its 88 original buildings (houses, shops, offices, inns, courthouse, jail, armory, Capitol, the works) and hiring a top-notch staff to run things so graciously, 21st-century hassles seem to disappear. We bought a package pass that admitted us to three Historic Triangle sites, which we visited in chronological order: Jamestown, Williamsburg, Yorktown (our pass also threw in nearby Busch Gardens and Water Country USA). Staying on **Colonial Williamsburg** property, we could walk in and out of the historic area, and at check-in we booked as many extras as we could from a crowded activity schedule. We had dinner in one of the taverns on-site (for reservations call ✆ **800/447-8679** or 757/229-2141), eating surprisingly delicious authentic dishes by candlelight with live minstrels strolling around. We watched an actor channel Patrick Henry for an hour, deftly answering the audience's every question. All the costumed interpreters stationed around the site are amazingly well-informed; some of them refuse to admit they aren't living in 1770 (almost a running joke with the visitors watching them), but others are more relaxed, like the cabinetmaker who jokingly asked us to bring him some Dunkin' Donuts. Even he had PhD-level knowledge of his era—not just cabinetry but agriculture, the colonial economy, and pre-Revolutionary politics. We were fascinated by our half-hour chat while he turned chair legs on his lathe.

Jamestown, the first permanent English settlement in the New World, was a great surprise: You can drive around the actual site, with ruins of the original buildings, but the kids got more out of the Jamestown Settlement reconstruction—they could really see the alarmingly tiny ships that brought the settlers from England in 1607, and the primitive stockaded settlement, scarcely more sophisticated than the replica Powhatan Indian village nearby. At **Yorktown,** where Washington won the final victory of the American Revolution in 1781, we drove around the battlefield route and explored a replica army camp. Next time we'll skip Busch Gardens, but **Water Country USA** (© 800/343-7946; www.watercountry usa.com) was a marvelous surprise, the perfect goofy way to end our history-packed 3 days.

ⓘ **Williamsburg Visitor Center,** 101A Visitor Center Dr., VA 132, south of U.S. 60 bypass (© **800/HISTORY** [447-8679] or 757/229-1000; www.colonialwilliamsburg.com). **Jamestown-Yorktown Foundation** (© **888/593-4682** or 757/253-4838; www.historyis fun.org).

✈ Newport News/Williamsburg International, 14 miles.

🛏 $$ **Crowne Plaza Williamsburg at Fort Magruder,** 6945 Pocahontas Trail (U.S. 60; © **800/496-7621** or 757/220-2250; www.cpwilliamsburghotel.com). $$ **Williamsburg Woodlands Hotel & Suites,** 105 Visitor Center Dr. (© **800/HISTORY** [447-8679] or 757/253-2277; www.colonialwilliamsburg.com).

WHY THEY'LL THANK YOU: Being extras in a history movie.

40

Philadelphia
Cradle of Liberty
All ages • Pennsylvania

IT'S NO EXAGGERATION TO CALL THIS THE MOST HISTORIC SQUARE MILE in America, the very place where the Declaration of Independence was signed and the Constitution of the United States hammered out. The look is tidy and stereotypical, steepled red-brick buildings with neat white porticos. Yet there's nothing tidy about what happened here—it took enormous courage for these British colonists to leap off this cliff—and when you see your child's eyes light up, realizing that these were real people and not just Faces on the Money, that's when you'll be glad you came to Philadelphia.

The focal point of Independence National Historical Park is **Independence Hall,** Chestnut Street between 5th and 6th streets, where the Second Continental Congress convened in a chamber known as the Pennsylvania Assembly Room in May 1775. Virginian Thomas Jefferson was assigned to write a document setting forth the colonists' grievances (Jefferson worked on it while boarding at **Graff House,** nearby at 7th and Market sts.), and by July 4, 1776, the Declaration of Independence was ready to be signed by the Congress—in Independence Hall you can even see the silver inkwell they used. You can also see the Rising Sun Chair that George Washington sat in 11 years later to preside over the Constitutional Convention, as President of the new United States. In a glass pavilion next door rests the 2,000-pound **Liberty Bell,** which was rung in 1776 at the first public reading of the Declaration; circle around it to find the famous crack up its side, which has been there since it was cast in 1751. At the northern end of grassy Independence Mall, the modern **National Constitution Center,** 525 Arch St., is so darn interactive, the children may not even notice how educational it is—you can take your own Presidential Oath of Office or try on a Supreme Court robe. In Signers' Hall, bronze life-size statues

The Liberty Bell.

depict the delegates who signed the Declaration—putting faces to those famous signatures was enormously satisfying.

And while you're here, follow Arch Street a few blocks east from the mall to the tiny **Betsy Ross House,** 239 Arch St. (© **215/629-4026;** www.betsyrosshouse.org), where a widowed Quaker seamstress supposedly sewed the first American flag. No one knows for sure if she really sewed it, or if this was even her house, but it makes a great story; and the house is so quaint, you'll want to believe it.

ⓘ **Visitor Center,** 6th and Market sts. (© **800/537-7676** or 215/965-7676; www.independencevisitorcenter.com).

✈ Philadelphia International.

🏨 $$ **Best Western Plus Independence Park Hotel,** 235 Chestnut St. (© **800/624-2988** or 215/922-4443; www.independence parkhotel.com). $$$ **Rittenhouse Hotel,** 210 W. Rittenhouse Sq. (© **800/635-1042** or 215/546-9000; www.rittenhousehotel.com).

WHY THEY'LL THANK YOU: Imagine John Hancock, dipping his quill pen in that inkwell.

The Statue of Liberty & Ellis Island

Gateway to America

Ages 6 & up • New York, New York

THE ICON TO END ALL ICONS, NEW YORK CITY'S AWE-INSPIRING Statue of Liberty is recognizable around the world as the symbol of American freedom. What's more, this is the city's greatest two-for-one deal: The same ferryboat takes you to the Ellis Island Immigration Museum, which turns out to be the real kid pleaser of the pair.

The **Statue of Liberty** (or, as she is officially known, *Liberty Enlightening the World*) is impressive enough from across the harbor, but close up—man, this chick is BIG. Don't be surprised if your young ones feel overwhelmed; even adults can get vertigo staring up her stately toga-clad physique. Lady Liberty weighs in at 225 tons of hammered copper, oxidized as planned to a delicate pale green, and her nose alone is 4½ feet long. Given to the United States by France, she has presided over the harbor since 1886 as a symbol of America's stature as a nation of immigrants. Beginning in late October 2011, the interior of the statue will be closed for yearlong renovations to upgrade stairways, elevators, and mechanical systems (visit www.nps.gov for up-to-date information). But even if you can't go inside, it's still worth the trip to stroll around Liberty Island and gaze out over the harbor.

From the mountain of ragtag luggage stacked right inside the front doors, upstairs to the cramped dormitories and medical examination rooms (cough the wrong way and you could be sent right back to Europe), to glass cases crammed with the family heirlooms immigrants brought with them, the **Ellis Island Immigration**

Profile of the Statue of Liberty.

Museum brings history to life. From 1892 to 1954, this was America's main immigration port of entry, where successive waves of new Americans first set foot on the soil of their new homeland. Prepare to be awed by the second-floor Registry Hall, its soaring vaulted ceiling faced with white tile, where new arrivals shuffled along in tediously long lines to be interviewed by immigration officials. (Cue up the theme from *The Godfather, Part II.*) On the Wall of Honor outside, some 420,000 immigrants' names are inscribed in steel. There are hands-on exhibits, films, live plays, computer stations where you can examine ship manifests—2 hours is barely enough to do this place justice.

Both sites are free, though you'll have to pay for the boat over. Ferryboats make frequent trips, running a 35-minute loop from Battery Park to Liberty Island to Ellis Island and back to Battery Park (from New Jersey you can board ferries in Liberty State Park).

ⓘ **Statue of Liberty,** Liberty Island (ⓒ **212/363-3200;** www.nps.gov/stli). **Ellis Island** (ⓒ **212/363-3200;** www.nps.gov/elis). **Ferry** (ⓒ **877/LADY-TIX** [523-9849] or 201/604-2800; www.statuecruises.com).

✈ John F. Kennedy International, Newark Liberty International, LaGuardia.

🛏 $$ **Excelsior Hotel,** 45 W. 81st St. (ⓒ **800/368-4575** or 212/362-9200; www.excelsiorhotelny.com). $$$ **Le Parker Meridien,** 119 W. 56th St. (pedestrian entrance: 118 W. 57th St.; ⓒ **800/543-4300** or 212/245-5000; www.parkermeridien.com).

WHY THEY'LL THANK YOU: America's beacon to the world still shines here.

Amish Country
The Plain People of Pennsylvania
All ages • Lancaster, Pennsylvania

ROLLING HILLS, WINDING CREEKS, NEATLY CULTIVATED FARMS, COVERED bridges—Lancaster County, Pennsylvania, has a bucolic beauty that would attract visitors anyway. But most tourists come here to see the Amish, dressed in their old-fashioned black clothes and driving buggies at a slow clip-clop along country roads. Yet these folks are not actors, they are real working people, and their strict customs are meant to separate them from the modern world, not to draw attention from it. The challenge of coming here with children is to discover the essence of the Amish community without falling into the tourist trap.

Begin in quaintly named Intercourse, Pennsylvania, at **The People's Place,** 3513 Old Philadelphia Pike (✆ **800/390-8436;** closed Sun), an interpretive center that will teach kids the subtle distinctions between three local sects: the Amish, the Mennonites, and the Brethren, who settled here in the early 18th century, drawn by William Penn's promise of religious tolerance. The children will learn, for example, not to take photos of the Amish, why Amish children attend school in one-room schoolhouses, and why the Amish paint hex designs on their barns. Avoiding Intercourse's gaggle of Pennsylvania-Dutch-themed shops, head west to Bird-in-Hand (another quirky name) for a 20-minute jaunt in a horse-drawn buggy at **Abe's Buggy Ride,** 2596 Old Philadelphia Pike (✆ **717/392-1794;** www.abesbuggyrides.com; closed Sun)—maybe this will help youngsters appreciate the slow pace of Amish life. Stop east of Lancaster for a guided tour of the 10-room **Amish Farm and House,** 2395 Lincoln Hwy. E. (U.S.30; ✆ **717/394-6185;** www.amishfarmandhouse.com). Wind up at the **Central Market** downtown, at 23 N. Market St. (just off Penn Sq.; ✆ **717/291-4723;** www.centralmarketlancaster.com; Tues and Fri–Sat only), the oldest farmers' market in the U.S., with its swirling fans, 1860-vintage tiles, and hitching posts.

In summer, tourists clog the main roads around Lancaster, and horse-drawn vehicles can cause bottlenecks; get a good area map so you can venture onto quiet back roads, where you have a better chance of seeing Amish farmers in their daily rounds. Stop at local farm stands to buy their excellent produce, and you'll have a natural opportunity to exchange a few words. Perhaps the best way to get the flavor of Amish life is to stay with a farm family: Contact the **Pennsylvania Dutch Convention & Visitors Bureau** (see below) for a list of working farms that take guests. Expect simple lodgings, hall bathrooms, and filling family-style breakfasts.

Buggy in Lancaster County.

ⓘ **Pennsylvania Dutch CVB,** 501 Greenfield Rd. (🕾 **800/PA-DUTCH** [723-8824] or 717/299-8901; www.padutchcountry.com). **Mennonite Information Center,** 2209 Millstream Rd. (🕾 **800/858-8320** or 717/299-0954; www.mennoniteinfoctr.com).

✈ Philadelphia International, 57 miles.

🛏 $$ **Country Inn of Lancaster,** 2133 Lincoln Hwy. E. (U.S. 30; 🕾 **877/393-3413** or 717/393-3413; www.countryinnoflancaster. com). $$$ **Willow Valley Inn & Suites,** 2416 Willow St. Pike (🕾 **800/444-1714;** www.willowvalley.com).

BEST TIME: Monday to Saturday, as many Amish attractions are closed Sunday.

WHY THEY'LL THANK YOU: Discovering that the Plain People are human too.

Mystic Seaport
Salty Thrill of a Vintage Shipyard
Ages 6 & up • Mystic, Connecticut

NOWADAYS, THE IDEA OF KILLING A WHALE IS SHOCKING TO MOST— yet for many years of the 19th century, when whales were much more plentiful, whale oil was an important commodity (not to mention whalebone for ladies' corsets), and towns all along the New England coast prospered on the whaling industry. That's the sliver of history preserved at this open-air village in Mystic, Connecticut. Standing on the Seaport's re-created waterfront, we gazed out across the wide estuary of the Mystic River and found it just about impossible not to feel the lure of the open sea.

The heart of the Seaport's collection is an ever-growing cache of some 500 ships, 2 centuries' worth of seagoing vessels, powered by everything from oars and sails to steam paddle wheels and engines. Rather than adhering to one historic period, Mystic Seaport adheres to its nautical theme. Yes, there are the requisite print ship, cooperage, schoolhouse, general store, and tavern, but the 17-acre site also features a ropewalk, a boat shed, a sail loft, a rigging loft, a lifesaving station, even shops for ship carvers and makers of nautical instruments. Staff members working in these shops aren't dressed in costumes and they aren't actors; they are real experts in the crafts they demonstrate, and delighted to share their knowledge with visitors. Somehow this makes the site feel more authentic, not less.

The most important ships in the collection have been designated national landmarks: the three-masted square-rigged whaler ***Charles W. Morgan*** (1841); the 1866 sloop smack ***Emma C. Berry,*** a graceful wood-hulled fishing boat; the 1908 paddle-wheeled excursion steamer ***Sabino;*** and the 1921 two-masted fishing schooner ***L. A. Dunton.*** But the one that my kids found most fascinating to climb aboard was the replica of the impossibly cramped slave

Mystic Seaport.

trade schooner **Amistad,** which was re-created right here in the Seaport's restoration workshops. Museum buildings on-site display extensive collections of things like scrimshaw and ship models and figureheads. A variety of boat trips are offered; inquire at the desk when you arrive, because once you've wandered around the site for a while, the urge to get out on the water becomes pretty strong. When you exit for the day, ask the gatekeeper to validate your ticket so you can come back the next day for free.

ⓘ 75 Greenmanville Ave. (CT 27; ✆ **888/973-2767** or 860/572-5315; www.mysticseaport.org).

✈ Providence T. F. Green International, 45 miles.

🛏 $$ **Hilton Mystic,** 20 Coogan Blvd. (✆ **800/445-8667** or 860/572-0731; www.hiltonmystic.com).

WHY THEY'LL THANK YOU: Going down to the sea in ships.

Stockyards National Historic District

Where Cowpokes Cut Loose

All ages • Fort Worth, Texas

FORT WORTH SURE DOES PUT THE "COW" IN "COWBOYS." WHEN THIS town boomed in the 1890s, it was because it had the Southwest's biggest livestock market, where millions of cattle—as well as horses, mules, hogs, and sheep—were shipped north along the Chisholm Trail. That's how Fort Worth got the nickname "Cow-town," and the Stockyards are where the city's Old West heritage burns brightest.

Two miles north of downtown Fort Worth, the 125-acre Stock-yards District, with its Spanish-flavored architecture, is still a lively place to hang out—only now it's tourists, not cattlemen, thronging the sidewalks along Exchange Street. Commercial it may be, but its robust Western vibe is infectious. Twice a day, at 11:30am and 4pm, duded-up cowhands drive about 15 head of longhorn steers down the red-brick street past the Stockyards. Former hog and sheep pens have been turned into **Stockyards Station,** a festival mall of Western-themed shops and restaurants, where the city's most authentic boots and Stetson hats are for sale. The old horse and mule barns have been turned into the **Texas Cowboy Hall of Fame,** 128 E. Exchange Ave. (© **817/626-7131;** www.texascowboy halloffame.com), a magnet for rodeo fans. Inside the **Livestock Exchange Building,** 131 E. Exchange Ave., the nerve center of the old livestock business, the small **Stockyards Museum** (© **817/ 625-5082;** www.stockyardsmuseum.org) displays artifacts such as guns, barbed wire, furniture, and clothing. Western music and movie stars, such as Gene Autry, Dale Evans, Roy Rogers, and Bob Wills, are honored in bronze along Exchange Avenue's **Trail of Fame.**

Keeping the kids busy around here is no problemo. Across from Stockyards Station, they can get lost in the **Cowtown Cattlepen Maze,** 145 E. Exchange Ave. (✆ **817/624-6666;** www.cowtown cattlepenmaze.com), a wooden labyrinth built to look like cattle pens. The **Grapevine Vintage Railroad** (✆ 817/410-3123; www. gvrr.com) runs two different daily routes from the Stockyards, one to downtown Fort Worth, the other out to Grapevine, Texas. The **Stockyards' Arena & Livery,** 128 E. Exchange Ave. (✆ **817/624-3446**), offers guided horseback rides out along the Trinity River. On most weekend nights, there's rodeo action at the **Cowtown Coliseum,** 121 E. Exchange Ave. (✆ **817/625-1025;** www.cowtown coliseum.com), the world's first indoor rodeo arena. **Billy Bob's Texas,** 2520 Rodeo Plaza (✆ **817/624-7117;** www.billybobstexas. com), known as the world's largest honky-tonk, offers families line-dancing lessons every Thursday evening.

ⓘ 130 E. Exchange Ave. (✆ **817/624-4741;** www.fortworthstock yards.org).

✈ Dallas–Fort Worth International.

🛏 $ **Residence Inn Fort Worth University,** 1701 S. University Dr., Ft. Worth (✆ **888/236-2427** or 817/870-1011; www.marriott. com/hotels/travel/dfwrp). $$$ **Stockyards Hotel,** 109 E. Exchange Ave., Ft. Worth (✆ **800/423-8471** or 817/625-6427; www.stock yardshotel.com).

WHY THEY'LL THANK YOU: Yee-HAW! That durn cattle drive.

California Gold Rush Country
Land of the Forty-Niners
Ages 6 & up • Hwy. 49 from Nevada City to Angels Camp

IN A CAVERN, IN A CANYON, EXCAVATING FOR A MINE / LIVED A MINER, forty-niner . . . Rarely do state highway numbers have historical significance, but **California State Hwy. 49** does. Winding through the hills west of Sacramento, **CA 49** is the main road through a string of Wild West towns that sprang up overnight in the California Gold Rush of 1849. As if frozen in time, their Main Streets still have raised wooden sidewalks, buildings with double porches, saloons, and Victorian storefronts. Touring the Gold Country, the kids will feel transplanted to a movie western (hundreds of films have been shot here), to a time when the promise of an easy fortune lured thousands of adventurers to risk their all in a raw new territory. Soon enough the boom went bust—but not before it had jump-started the settlement of the whole West Coast.

It's about 100 miles along CA 49 from Nevada City in the north to Angels Camp in the south; visiting the whole area could take several days. Here are the highlights: Start where the Gold Rush itself began—just north of Placerville in quiet, pretty **Coloma** at the **Marshall Gold Discovery State Historic Park** (© **530/622-3470**; www.coloma.com/gold). Here, on the south fork of the American River, on January 24, 1848, carpenter James Marshall was building John Sutter's sawmill when he chanced upon a gold nugget. On Main Street, the largest building in town is a replica of the sawmill; exhibits at the **Gold Discovery Museum** lay out the story of the frenzy that ensued once the news got out. Notice the number of Chinese stores on Main Street, the remnants of a once-sizable community of Chinese who immigrated here to provide labor for the mines.

Some 40 miles south of here, you can tour the **Sutter Gold Mine,** 13660 CA 49, Sutter Creek (ⓒ **866/762-2837** or 209/736-2708; www.suttergold.com). You'll wear a hard hat, ride on a mining shuttle, and "tag in" just like a miner. Down in the shaft, you may be able to spot gemstones and gold deposits still embedded in the quartz of the Comet Vein. The other face of the Gold Rush shows at two nearby ghost towns—**Mokelumne Hill,** nowadays one street overlooking a valley with a few old buildings, and decrepit **Volcano,** which looks almost haunted with the dark rock and blind window frames of a few backless, ivy-covered buildings. Once it had a population of 8,000; today, it's more like 100. That's what happens when a boom goes bust.

Another 30 miles farther south, Gold Rush country's most popular site, **Columbia State Historic Park,** 22708 Broadway, Columbia (ⓒ **209/588-9128;** www.columbiacalifornia.com), re-creates a boom town at its lively height. Kids love roaming around its dusty car-free streets, where they can take stagecoach rides or visit a newspaper office, a blacksmith's forge, a Wells Fargo express office, or a Victorian-era saloon.

ⓘ www.historichwy49.com.

✈ Sacramento International, 55 miles from Placerville.

🛏 $$ **City Hotel,** 22768 Main St., Columbia State Historic Park (ⓒ **800/444-7275** or 209/532-1479; www.cityhotel.com). $$ **Imperial Hotel,** 14202 CA 49, Amador City (ⓒ **209/267-9172;** www.imperialamador.com).

WHY THEY'LL THANK YOU: Gold fever and ghost towns.

46

National Museum of the American Indian

Ages 6 & up • Washington, D.C.

AMONG THE STATELY WHITE STONE PALACES LINING THE NATIONAL Mall, this Smithsonian branch really stands out: A burnt sand-colored exterior of kasota limestone wraps around undulating walls, echoing the pueblos and hogans of the Southwest tribes. With its bands of reflective windows peering out like eagle eyes, it reminds me of some sort of Northwest tribal totem. Inside, a huge rotunda lobby is filled with celestial references, from the equinoxes and solstices mapped on the floor to the sky visible in the oculus dome, 120 feet overhead, and nature is brought in throughout the galleries—wonderfully appropriate for a museum celebrating Native peoples.

As one of the Smithsonian's newest branches, the American Indian museum shakes off the dusty approaches of the past and has so much more than just exhibits in glass cases. Of course, it has an amazing number of artifacts to display, with its core collection of 800,000 **Native American artifacts**—wood and stone carvings, masks, pottery, feather bonnets, and so on, representing some 1,000 Native communities through North and South America. Children can be lost for minutes studying some of these intricate handmade objects. While there are many fine museums showcasing one tribal group or another, this one includes all the native populations of the Western Hemisphere, and many of the exhibits are organized around cross-cultural themes. (Never before had I noticed so many connections between North and South American tribes.)

The museum's designers also purposely made this a "living" museum, with Native peoples performing, storytelling, and displaying their own art alongside the historic exhibits—that fabulous atrium entrance turns out to be perfect for **ceremonial dances.** Workshops include **demonstrations** of traditional arts such as weaving or basket making; a roster of **films** includes a number of animated shorts that retell nature legends and creation myths.

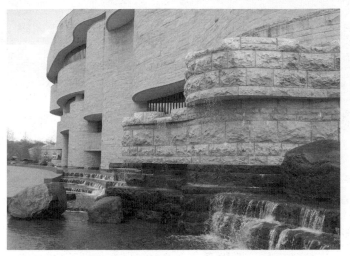

National Museum of the American Indian.

Almost every exhibit, it seems, has a video of some tribe member explaining the significance of this or that custom—a much easier way for kids to learn than reading blocks of text mounted on a wall. Again, how appropriate for a Native American museum to honor oral tradition.

Some of the exhibit themes are a bit too anthropological, or too politically complex, for children to follow, but just looking at the precious objects can be enough. A pair of traditional beaded moccasins alongside red high-top sneakers hand-painted with tribal motifs—that's the sort of thing kids intuitively get.

ⓘ 4th St. and Independence Ave. SW (✆ **202/633-1000;** www. nmai.si.edu).

✈ Ronald Reagan Washington National, 5 miles. Washington Dulles International, 26 miles. Baltimore/Washington International Thurgood Marshall, 30 miles.

🛏 $$ **Embassy Suites,** 1250 22nd St. NW (✆ **800/EMBASSY** [362-2779] or 202/857-3388; www.embassysuites.com). $$ **Georgetown Suites,** 1000 29th St. NW & 1111 30th St. NW, Georgetown (✆ **800/348-7203** or 202/298-7800; www.georgetownsuites.com).

WHY THEY'LL THANK YOU: Seeing what life's like for children of the tribe.

Black History **47**

Black Heritage Trail

All ages • Boston, Massachusetts

MANY TOURISTS DON'T REALIZE THAT BOSTON HAS NOT ONE BUT TWO Freedom Trails—the Revolutionary War trail, and the Black Heritage Trail, which celebrates Boston's antislavery movement. The latter runs 1.6 miles, through Beacon Hill, the center of the free black community in the years leading up to the Civil War. Walking around this neighborhood, you get a sense of how a close-knit black community developed, gradually cultivating political savvy and spreading radical new ideas. The seeds of the Emancipation Proclamation were sown here on Beacon Hill. Walking the Trail is a great way to explore an era of American history that all too often takes a back seat in Revolutionary War–obsessed New England.

The 15 marked points on the trail start at the **Robert Gould Shaw Memorial** on Beacon Street across from the State House. Shaw was the white officer who led the 54th Massachusetts Regiment, the Union's first black regiment, celebrated in the 1989 film *Glory*, and this bas-relief sculpture by Augustus Saint-Gaudens is incredibly affecting. Other buildings you'll pass include the homes of George Middleton, an African-American Revolutionary War soldier; successful barber John J. Smith, a free black who hosted antislavery debates both at his shop and in his home; and Lewis Hayden, a freed slave whose boardinghouse was an early

Underground Railroad stop. You'll see the Baptist church where church desegregation efforts began in the 1830s (years later, after the Civil War, the same church building became Boston's first African Methodist Episcopal church).

From Memorial Day to Labor Day, National Park Service rangers lead free 2-hour **guided tours** daily along the route; the rest of the year, contact the Park Service to arrange a tour. To go at your own pace without the commentary, pick up a brochure outlining the tour at the Boston Common and State Street visitor kiosks, or from the **Museum of African American History,** 46 Joy St. (© **617/ 725-0022;** www.afroammuseum.org), which is where the Trail ends. The museum's site occupies the restored **Abiel Smith School** (1834), the first American public grammar school for African-American children, and the **African Meeting House** (1806), the oldest standing black church in the United States. William Lloyd Garrison founded the New England Anti-Slavery Society in this building, where Frederick Douglass made some of his great abolitionist speeches. Once known as the "Black Faneuil Hall," it also schedules lectures, concerts, and church meetings. The museum's displays employ art, artifacts, documents, historic photographs, and other objects—including many family heirlooms. Children enjoy the interactive touch-screen displays and multimedia presentations, and the patient, enthusiastic staff helps them put the exhibits in context.

ⓘ © **617/742-5415;** www.nps.gov/boaf.

✈ Boston Logan International.

🛏 $$ **DoubleTree Suites by Hilton,** 400 Soldiers Field Rd. (© **800/222-TREE** [8733] or 617/783-0090; www.doubletree.com). $ **The Midtown Hotel,** 220 Huntington Ave. (© **800/343-1177** or 617/262-1000; www.midtownhotel.com).

WHY THEY'LL THANK YOU: A second Freedom Trail, just as important as the first.

Dr. King's Legacy

Ages 6 & up • Atlanta, Georgia

The civil rights leader Martin Luther King, Jr., is by any measure a great man. In his hometown of Atlanta, Georgia, the 10-block area around Auburn Avenue is one of the city's most-visited sites, encompassing King's boyhood home and the Baptist church where King, his father, and his grandfather were all ministers. While other civil rights sites may illuminate the issues of that tumultuous era better, this is the place where you'll really get a feeling for this complex, gifted man who dared to change history.

To me the real heart of the site is the historic buildings associated with King. Start out at the gracefully landscaped **visitor center,** where you can book tours of the sites (get here early in the day, at least in summer, because tickets do run out) and get up to speed on King's life and times with audiovisual programs and exhibits. First off is the **Birth Home of Dr. Martin Luther King, Jr.,** 501 Auburn Ave. (✆ 404/331-6922), the modest Queen Anne–style house where Martin Luther King, Jr., was born on January 15, 1929, and lived until he was 12. The house has been restored to its appearance when young Martin lived here—even the linoleum is an authentic reproduction, and a good deal of King memorabilia is displayed. His father (Martin Luther King, Sr., obviously) was a Baptist minister and pastor of the **Ebenezer Baptist Church** down the street at 407 Auburn Ave. (✆ 404/688-7300), a Gothic Revival–style church founded in 1886 and completed in 1922. Years later, from 1960 to 1968—at the height of the civil rights struggle—Martin Luther King, Jr., served as his father's co-pastor here, the two actively using their pulpit to press for social change. The National Park Service operates it as a living museum, with guided weekday tours, periodic church services, and a monthly choir performance. In nearby **Freedom Plaza** rests Dr. King's white marble crypt, surrounded by a five-tiered reflecting pool.

The district is somewhat dominated by the hulking modern **King Center,** 449 Auburn Ave. (✆ 404/526-8900; www.thekingcenter.

org), a memorial and educational center directed by King's son. It has a huge library and archives on the civil rights movement, including Dr. King's personal papers, but many visitors are most interested in the exhibition hall, where selected memorabilia of King and the civil rights movement are displayed. You can see his Bible and clerical robe and a handwritten sermon; on a grim note, there's the suit King was wearing when a deranged woman stabbed him in New York City, as well as the key to his room at the Lorraine Motel in Memphis, Tennessee, where he was assassinated. The best reason to come here is to settle down in the Screening Room to watch videos of Dr. King's most stirring sermons and speeches, including "I Have a Dream." The man's words still move us.

(i) **MLK, Jr., National Historic Site,** John Wesley Dobbs Ave. NE (© **404/331-6922;** www.nps.gov/malu).

✈ Hartsfield-Jackson Atlanta International.

🛏 $$$ **The Georgian Terrace Hotel,** 659 Peachtree St., Atlanta (© **800/651-2316** or 404/897-1991; www.thegeorgian terrace.com). $$ **Marriott Stone Mountain Inn,** 1058 Robert E. Lee Dr., Stone Mountain (© **888/236-2427** or 770/469-3311; www. marriott.com/atlsi).

WHY THEY'LL THANK YOU: The "I Have a Dream" speech.

49   **Black History**

Alabama's Civil Rights Trail

Ages 8 & up • Montgomery, Birmingham & Selma, Alabama

WHAT SEEMS LIKE YESTERDAY'S HEADLINES TO US GROWN-UPS IS IN fact the foggy past to our kids. Take, for example, that afternoon in 1955 when a black seamstress named Rosa Parks was arrested for not yielding her seat to a white man on a Montgomery, Alabama, public bus. A controversial bus boycott followed (led by a young

Rev. Martin Luther King, Jr.), one of the first skirmishes in the civil rights battle of the 1960s. We refer to it so casually, as if everyone should know about this tumultuous era, but it's all new to the kids—and even adults may find they didn't know as much as they thought.

That 1955 street scene is re-created at Montgomery's **Rosa Parks Library and Museum,** 252 Montgomery St. (© 334/241-8661; http://montgomery.troy.edu/rosaparks/museum), with a replica of the bus Parks rode, video images, and a multimedia tableau. Wonderful interactive displays throughout the museum engage children in Parks's inspiring life as an activist. King's role, of course, was pivotal, as you'll learn on the guided tour of the neat **Dexter Avenue King Memorial Baptist Church,** 454 Dexter Ave. (© **334/263-3970;** www.dexterkingmemorial.org), where King used his pulpit to press for social change. Even more evocative is the **Dexter Parsonage Museum,** 309 S. Jackson St. (© **334/261-3270;** www.dexterkingmemorial.org), a simple white bungalow that's been furnished as it was in the 1950s, when King and his family lived here: You can see the study where he wrote his sermons, the dining room where activists met to plan the boycott, and a front window shattered by a bomb meant to scare King off his campaign. Downtown, the black granite **Civil Rights Memorial,** 400 Washington Ave., designed by Maya Lin, pays tribute to those who fought for racial equality.

You have to credit Alabama for embracing this anguished chapter of its past. Birmingham, 90 miles north of Montgomery, has an entire downtown district memorializing civil rights events: engrossing displays (segregated water fountains, a bombed-out bus, King's jail cell) in the **Birmingham Civil Rights Institute,** 520 16th St. N. (© **205/328-9696;** www.bcri.org); the historic **16th St. Baptist Church,** 1530 6th Ave. N. (© **205/251-9402;** www.16thstreet baptist.org), where a 1963 bombing by the Ku Klux Klan killed four girls; and outdoor **Kelly Ingram Park,** where a paved Freedom Path recounts crucial events with plaques and sculptures. An hour's drive west of Montgomery in Selma, you can see the **Edmund Pettus Bridge,** site of the 1965 "Bloody Sunday" riot, where a voting-rights protest march met brutal resistance from police and local vigilantes, and then stop in the **National Voting Rights Museum,** 6 U.S. 80 E. (© **334/418-0800;** www.nvrm.org), which displays artifacts about voter-registration campaigns—just one phase of the war for civil rights in America.

(i) **Sweet Home Alabama** (www.touralabama.org).

✈ Birmingham-Shuttlesworth International, 90 miles to Montgomery.

🛏 $$ **Embassy Suites Montgomery,** 300 Tallapoosa St., Montgomery (✆ **334/269-5055;** www.embassysuites.com). $$$ **The Redmont,** 2101 Fifth Ave. N., Birmingham (✆ **877/536-2085** or 205/324-2101; www.theredmont.com).

WHY THEY'LL THANK YOU: Dr. King had a dream.

---

50 Science Museums

American Museum of Natural History
Discovering Dinosaurs
All ages • New York, New York

How many children have fallen in love with dinosaurs in the echoing galleries of this world-class New York City museum? And the dinosaurs are only the tip of the iceberg: Over the years, Holden Caulfield brooded over its collection of Northwest Indian totem poles in *The Catcher in the Rye;* in the planetarium, Woody Allen wooed Diane Keaton in the 1979 film *Manhattan;* and curious scientists plunked Darryl Hannah's mermaid into a tank to examine her in the 1984 movie *Splash.* It's one of America's great museums, and invariably engrossing for children.

When you enter the magnificent rotunda at the top of the Central Park West steps—named for Theodore Roosevelt, the outdoors-loving President who helped found the museum—a rearing skeleton of a mommy dinosaur protecting her baby from a small, fierce predator clues you in that the dazzling interactive fourth-floor dinosaur halls are the perennial star attraction. But our favorite sights are the superb dioramas in the **Hall of North American Mammals**—the grizzly bear raking open a freshly caught salmon,

The Hall of African Mammals at the American Museum of Natural History.

majestic elks lifting their massive antlers, wolves loping through eerie nighttime snow—or, on the floor above, the bi-level **Hall of African Mammals,** where you can circle around a lumbering herd of perfectly preserved elephants or check out the giraffes browsing by their water hole. In the dimly lit **Milstein Hall of Ocean Life,** a gargantuan model of a blue whale swims overhead while dolphins arc through plastic waves. Around the corner, the less-well-visited **Hall of North American Forests** dioramas are our family secret—a peaceful part of the museum where you can hunt for blue jays in oak trees and rattlesnakes behind the cactus. Haunting music playing in the **African** and **Asian peoples** sections lull you into studying precisely detailed displays of cultural artifacts: a Chinese bride's ornate sedan chair, a pygmy's blow darts, a re-creation of a Siberian shaman healing rite, a Yoruba ceremonial costume made of red snail shells.

The stunning **Rose Center for Earth and Space,** a 95-foot-high glass cube, includes an interactive exhibit on the nature of the universe, where you can step on a scale that shows your weight on Saturn, see an eerie phosphorescent model of the expanding universe, and touch cosmic debris. There are an IMAX theater, a space show, and always at least a couple of traveling exhibitions (my only quibble with the museum is the substantial extra fees charged for these, on top of an already hefty admission price). But there's enough to do here that you don't need to go for the extras. Wander at will, keeping your eyes open and your imagination at the ready. It's a magical place.

(i) Central Park West and 79th St. (© **212/769-5100;** www.amnh. org).

✈ John F. Kennedy International, 15 miles. Newark Liberty International, 16 miles. LaGuardia, 8 miles.

🛏 $$ **Excelsior Hotel,** 45 W. 81st St. (© **800/368-4575** or 212/ 362-9200; www.excelsiorhotelny.com). $$$ **Le Parker Meridien,** 119 W. 56th St. (pedestrian entrance: 118 W. 57th St.; © **800/543-4300** or 212/245-5000; www.parkermeridien.com).

WHY THEY'LL THANK YOU: The dioramas and the dinosaurs.

Franklin Institute
In the Spirit of Old Ben Himself
Ages 4 & up • Philadelphia, Pennsylvania

Let's never forget that Benjamin Franklin was a scientist as well as a statesman, publisher, and philosopher: The Franklin stove and bifocal glasses were just two contraptions he invented, and of course there's that whole experiment with the kite in the thunderstorm. It warms my heart to visit the Franklin Institute in Philadelphia, which pays homage to the quirkiest of our Founding Fathers. At the core of this museum is the **Franklin National Memorial,** with a 30-ton statue of its namesake and an evocative hands-on gallery on Franklin's inventions and the scientists he inspired. While it looks all stately and neoclassical on the outside, however, this place wouldn't reflect the spirit of Franklin if it didn't have a fascinating clutter of other exhibits that simply encourage kids to putter around.

Hands-on is the watchword at the Franklin Institute; pick up a schedule of the museum staff's frequent **daily demonstrations** so you won't miss the fun stuff. The collection of science- and technology-oriented exhibits ranges from a gigantic walk-through heart to the Train Factory, where you can play engineer for a 350-ton locomotive, to a Van de Graaff generator that'll make your hair stand on end at the Electricity gallery. Kid Science, on the lower level, uses a dramatic anime-like storyline to teach basic science concepts to children ages 5 to 8. On the third floor, Sir Isaac's Loft demonstrates the principles of Newtonian physics with Rube Goldberg–ian machines, noisemakers, and light shows. The Sports Challenge section was intriguing, looking at the science behind popular sports like surfing and rock climbing, and we couldn't resist the Sky Bike, which you can ride along a 1-inch cable three stories above the atrium floor. The whole museum is all about curiosity, and it's one of the best embodiments of the scientific method you'll ever play in.

In the warmer months, a great **high-tech playground** sprouts out on the lawn, where young kids can really mess around with science concepts—the step-on organ is a crowd pleaser, as are the maze and the high-wire tandem bicycle. If your kids like this kind of stuff, you'll probably also want to devote some time to the **Please Touch Museum,** just a short drive away in Fairmount Park.

ⓘ **Franklin Institute,** Logan Circle, 20th St. and Benjamin Franklin Pkwy. (✆ **215/448-1200;** www.fi.edu). **Please Touch Museum,** 4231 Ave. of the Republic (✆ **215/581-3181;** www.pleasetouch museum.org).

✈ Philadelphia International.

🛏 $$ **Best Western Plus Independence Park Hotel,** 235 Chestnut St. (✆ **800/624-2988** or 215/922-4443; www.independence parkhotel.com). $$$ **Rittenhouse Hotel,** 210 W. Rittenhouse Sq. (✆ **800/635-1042** or 215/546-9000; www.rittenhousehotel.com).

WHY THEY'LL THANK YOU: Playing with electricity at Ben Franklin's museum.

52 Science Museums

The Exploratorium
The Ultimate Hands-On Museum
All ages • San Francisco, California

"THE BEST SCIENCE MUSEUM IN THE WORLD" IS WHAT *SCIENTIFIC American* magazine once called this San Francisco attraction, right by the waterfront parks of the Marina District. Set in a sprawling former airplane hangar, every bit of floor space is taken up with inventive activity stations and displays that just cry out for young-sters to press, jiggle, squeeze, fiddle, poke, and manipulate to their heart's content. I've been there with toddlers and I've been there with teens, and everyone has always been totally absorbed. They don't seem to care that they're also learning scientific concepts, in a way that will really stick.

The Exploratorium staff is constantly engaged in dreaming up new exhibits, so there's no guarantee that the stuff we loved won't have been replaced by something even cooler by the time you get there. The giant soap-bubble maker is perennially popular, as is the shadow wall, the visual distortion room, and machines that make sand patterns with sound waves. The **Tactile Dome** is an amazing experience for older kids, where they grope their way around in complete darkness, dependent on senses other than sight. Across Marina Boulevard, at the end of the Marina breakwater, you'll find one of the Exploratorium's most intriguing inventions: the **Wave Organ,** a hunk of concrete embedded with listening tubes that lead underwater to translate the ebb and flow of ocean currents into strange gurgles and humming sounds.

There's a handmade quality to many of the displays that I find very appealing—clearly they've been bolted and knocked together out of plywood, wires, PVC pipes, whatever is on hand, and I can't help but think this encourages kids to become putterers and inventors themselves. As my kids get older, their interests change; the last time we were there, they gravitated to exhibits on principles of light, optics, and perception, whereas in years past they were engrossed in the simple physics concepts demonstrated in the section on matter. Biology and electricity sections on the mezzanine are fascinating too. (There's a **play area** for under-4s, a godsend if you need to entertain a toddler while your older kid works the

The Exploratorium from across the pond.

exhibits.) On our most recent visit, I watched my continually squab-bling son and daughter sit for 15 minutes on either side of a mir-rored pane of glass, watching their grinning faces blend together as lighting levels were gradually raised and lowered—so much for hating your siblings.

You'll find local youngsters here, not just tourists and bored school groups. It's a noisy, high-raftered, under-lit space and even-tually we hit overload and have to bail out. But we never leave because we've run out of things to do.

(ⓘ) 3601 Lyon St. (℡ **415/397-5673;** www.exploratorium.org). **San Francisco Municipal Transportation Agency** (www.sfmta. com). **San Francisco Travel Association,** 900 Market St. (℡ **415/ 391-2000;** www.sanfrancisco.travel).

✈ San Francisco International, 13 miles. Oakland International, 18 miles.

🛏 $$$ **Argonaut Hotel,** 495 Jefferson St. (℡ **866/415-0704** or 415/563-0800; www.argonauthotel.com). $$ **Larkspur Hotel,** 524 Sutter St. (℡ **866/823-4669** or 415/421-2865; www.larkspurhotel unionsquare.com).

WHY THEY'LL THANK YOU: Hands-on = brains on.

53 The History of Flight

Kitty Hawk
The Wright Brothers Learn to Fly
Ages 4 & up • Kill Devil Hills, North Carolina

THE NAME KITTY HAWK IS FOREVER ASSOCIATED WITH ORVILLE AND Wilbur Wright—it says so right on North Carolina's license plates. That's the place where, on December 17, 1903, this brother-brother team from Dayton, Ohio, achieved the world's first sus-tained, controlled, heavier-than-air powered flight. (You need all those adjectives to distinguish the Wrights' flight from a mere glider or hot-air balloon flight.) But you could score big trivia points for knowing that the Wrights didn't take off from the town of Kitty Hawk, but from a nearby 90-foot-high dune called **Kill Devil Hill** on the Outer Banks, a bony finger of land that separates the Atlantic Ocean from the inner sounds and estuaries of North Carolina's coast. Ask the kids: If you were flying an experimental aircraft into the teeth of gusting Atlantic winds, would you really want to launch from a place called Kill Devil Hill?

Desperate to get home to Dayton in time for Christmas, Orville and Wilbur did get the Wright Flyer off the ground that windy December day in 1903, keeping it aloft for 59 seconds and flying a distance of 852 feet. Their feat is commemorated at the **Wright Brothers National Memorial,** an imposing 60-foot-high pylon of white North Carolina granite, erected in 1932 on Kill Devil Hill. In fact, the Wrights made four successful flights that day, of increasing lengths; numbered markers on the long slopes show how far

A glider at the Wright Brothers National Memorial.

they made it each time, until on the fourth go the Wright Flyer crash-landed. The visitor center features a replica of that **Wright Flyer,** plus a glider they flew here in 1902, along with a few exhibits telling the Wright Brothers' story; park rangers lead twice-daily tours, present talks at the visitor center, and run afternoon family activities such as kite flying or paper-airplane building. You can explore reconstructions of the hangar Orville and Wilbur built for their plane and their workshop/living quarters. The main thing, though, is to stand on the big grassy dune and feel the breezes rise off the water; it suddenly becomes clear why the Wright brothers traveled all the way to North Carolina to get their spidery winged craft aloft.

Not far away, at the highest sand dune on the East Coast, 138-foot-high Jockey's Ridge, you can try out those Outer Banks winds yourself by taking a hang-gliding lesson from the world's largest hang-gliding school, **Kitty Hawk Kites,** near the visitor center of **Jockey's Ridge State Park** (milepost 12 off U.S. 158 Bypass; ✆ **252/441-7132**). Beginning, intermediate, and advanced instruction are provided; for reservations, call ✆ **877/359-8447** or 252/441-2426; or go to www.kittyhawk.com.

ⓘ Milepost 7.5, U.S. 158 Bypass (✆ **252/441-7430;** www.nps.gov/wrbr).

✈ Norfolk International, VA, 80 miles.

🛏 $$ **Cahoons Cottages,** 7213 S. Virginia Dare Trail, Milepost 16.5, Nags Head (✆ **252/441-5358;** www.cahoonscottages.com). $$$ **The Tranquil House Inn,** 405 Queen Elizabeth Ave., Manteo (✆ **800/458-7069;** www.1587.com).

WHY THEY'LL THANK YOU: Feeling the wind beneath their wings.

National Air and Space Museum

Plane Fantastic

All ages • Washington, D.C.

The one do-not-miss stop for families visiting our nation's capital, Air and Space is pretty much the star player on the Smithsonian museum team, at least as far as kids are concerned. I still catch my breath when I walk into its sleek entrance hall off the Mall and see all those **historic aircraft** dangling from the ceiling—the Wright brothers' historic 1903 Wright Flyer, Charles Lindbergh's *Spirit of St. Louis,* the *Enola Gay* bomber that devastated Hiroshima, the *Friendship 7* capsule that took John Glenn into space. Jaded as I am by IMAX movies, I made a point of having my kids sit through the classic *To Fly!,* still my favorite of the genre; we spent another afternoon out in Virginia at the satellite location so we could see the space shuttle *Enterprise.* Whether you come here for the history, the science, or just the techno-thrill of seeing so much heavy metal, Air and Space delivers the goods.

Air and Space holds the largest collection of historic aircraft and spacecraft in the world; only about 10% of what it owns is actually on display, even with the annex out in Virginia. Besides gawking at the famous planes hanging out in the lobby, kids love to walk through the **Skylab orbital workshop;** other galleries highlight the solar system, U.S. manned spaceflights, and aviation during both world wars. You can sneak in some hard science education with **How Things Fly,** an interactive exhibit that demonstrates principles of flight and aerodynamics (the wind and smoke tunnels are especially fun), and get into some heady astrophysics with **Explore the Universe,** which probes theories about how the universe took shape. But this big, noisy, kid-packed museum isn't the sort of place where you want to be serious and thoughtful; besides the IMAX movie we wanted to do all the pumped-up extras like the **flight simulators** and the **space show** at the planetarium—admission to the museum is free, but very few families get away without buying a ticket for one of these add-ons.

The second part of the museum is out near Dulles Airport in Chantilly, Virginia, where two gigantic hangars—one for aviation artifacts, the other for space artifacts—accompany a 164-foot-tall **observation tower** for watching planes land and take off at Dulles. The **space hangar** is the length of three football fields—it has to be in order to house such huge artifacts as the space shuttle, rocket boosters, spacewalk capsules, and a full-scale prototype of the Mars Pathfinder lander. The scale of this technology is awesome, and you just can't appreciate it unless you stand right next to these babies and crane your neck upward.

(i) **National Mall Building,** Independence Ave. SW, between 4th and 7th sts. (✆ **202/633-2214;** www.nasm.si.edu). **Steven F. Udvar-Hazy Center,** 14390 Air and Space Museum Pkwy., Chantilly, VA (✆ **703/572-4118;** www.nasm.si.edu).

✈ Ronald Reagan Washington National, 5 miles. Washington Dulles International, 26 miles. Baltimore/Washington International Thurgood Marshall, 30 miles.

⨾ $$ **Embassy Suites,** 1250 22nd St. NW (✆ **800/EMBASSY** [362-2779] or 202/857-3388; www.embassysuites.com). $$ **Georgetown Suites,** 1000 29th St. NW & 1111 30th St. NW, Georgetown (✆ **800/348-7203** or 202/298-7800; www.georgetownsuites.com).

WHY THEY'LL THANK YOU: Historic flying machines soaring in the lobby.

Kennedy Space Center
10 . . . 9 . . . 8 . . .
Ages 4 & up • Titusville, Florida

Spaceflight has lost so much of its glamour that it can be hard for kids to comprehend how exciting it once was to watch a mighty booster rocket blast off from the launch pad at Cape Canaveral. So pop in a DVD of *The Right Stuff* or *Apollo 13* before your trip to the Space Coast. Make them see how being an astronaut was once the coolest job a kid could aspire to.

You don't have to be a space buff to be awed by the sheer grandeur of the facilities at NASA's primary space-launch facility. Begin your visit at the **Kennedy Space Center Visitor Complex**—though it's a bit theme-park-slick, it does outline the history of space exploration well, and there are real NASA rockets on display, as well as (the coolest thing to me) the actual Mercury Mission Control Room from the 1960s. Hands-on activities, a daily "encounter" with an astronaut, and an IMAX theater make this a place where kids will want to hang out. The **Astronaut Hall of Fame,** a separate attraction at the center, pays tribute to the Mercury, Gemini, and Apollo space jockeys, along with even more vintage spacecraft—a Mercury 7 capsule, a Gemini training capsule, and an Apollo 14 command module—and several space-y simulator rides. Plan ahead (call ✆ **866/737-5235** for a reservation) to snag a **lunch with an astronaut**—even such greats as John Glenn, Jim Lovell, Walt Cunningham, and Jon McBride have taken their turns in this daily event.

Narrated **bus tours** depart every 15 minutes to explore the sprawling space-center grounds. Stops include the LC-39 Observation Gantry, with a dramatic 360-degree view over launch pads; the International Space Station Center, where scientists and engineers prepare additions to the space station now in orbit; and the Apollo/Saturn V Center, which includes artifacts (a moon rock to touch!), films, interactive exhibits, and the 363-foot-tall Saturn V, the most powerful U.S. rocket ever launched. It's not all Disney-fied, which in

The Kennedy Space Center.

my opinion is a plus, but if the kids get restless (especially given the typical Florida heat), you can hop on the next bus and move on.

The real thrill, of course, is to see a **rocket launch.** Although the final space shuttle launch took place in July 2011 and the shuttle program is now retired, you can still see a rocket launch if you're lucky; check www.kennedyspacecenter.com/events-launches. aspx for a schedule of upcoming takeoffs (always an iffy thing, depending on weather or equipment problems). Or view rocket launches the way the locals do: from the causeways leading to the islands and on U.S. 1 as it skirts the waterfront in Titusville.

(i) NASA Pkwy. (FL 405; (C) **321/449-4444** for info, 866/737-5235 for reservations; www.kennedyspacecenter.com).

✈ Melbourne International, 22 miles. Orlando International, 35 miles.

🛏 $$$ **DoubleTree by Hilton Cocoa Beach Oceanfront,** 2080 N. Atlantic Ave., Cocoa Beach ((C) **800/222-TREE** [8733] or 321/783-9222; www.cocoabeachdoubletree.com). $$ **Riverview Hotel,** 103 Flagler Ave., New Smyrna Beach ((C) **800/945-7416** or 386/428-5858; www.riverviewhotel.com).

WHY THEY'LL THANK YOU: Huge rockets up close.

Inventions & Industry **56**

Edison National Historical Park
The Light Bulbs Go On
Ages 6 & up • West Orange, New Jersey

"I ALWAYS INVENTED TO OBTAIN MONEY TO GO ON INVENTING," Thomas Edison once said. The romantic notion of a genius tinkering alone at night over a breakthrough invention? That wasn't Edison. Yes, he was a gifted chemist and visionary, but he was also a shrewd businessman who amassed a fortune. Touring the Edison

Laboratory Complex is a fascinating look at one of the most efficient R & D operations in history.

Though Edison's first lab was in Menlo Park, New Jersey, this larger West Orange complex was in operation for over 40 years and accounted for over half of his patents. Notice how closely the ivy-covered red-brick buildings are set together—Edison designed it this way so he wouldn't waste too much time scurrying from chemistry lab to machine shop to drafting room. The kids may be surprised to learn that, of the 1,093 patents credited to Edison—the most any American has ever obtained—many were actually invented by other scientists who worked for him. Walking around the restored lab complex, you can visualize his team of some 200 researchers, hired to refine and improve existing inventions. There were light bulbs before Edison's, but his was more reliable, long-lasting, and easy to manufacture; the telegraph, the phonograph, the stock ticker, the movie camera, and projector were all devices that other scientists pursued at the same time, but Edison's versions *worked better*. Another 10,000 workers in the attached factory (not part of the

Lab at the Edison National Historical Park.

historic site) then mass-produced these inventions for commercial sale—he controlled the entire cycle. Accessories, too—there's a music recording studio you can peek into, where Edison engineers made sure phonograph customers would have something to play on their new machines.

One mile from the lab complex, you can see the fruits of Edison's labors in **Glenmont,** a 29-room red Queen Anne–style mansion in Llewellyn Park which Edison bought for his second wife, Mina. All the original furnishings are here, reflecting the formal Victorian style of the era, with lots of ornate carved wood, damask wall coverings, and stained-glass windows; things get comfier upstairs in the family living room, where Edison's children sometimes helped him look up scientific references in shelves full of books. One thing's for sure: This was probably the first house in the neighborhood with a phonograph, let alone the Home Projecting Kinetoscope—the Edison children must have been very in demand for play dates.

(i) 211 Main St., at Lakeside Ave. ((C) **973/736-0550;** www.nps.gov/edis).

✈ Newark Liberty International, 15 miles.

🛏 $$ **Excelsior Hotel,** 45 W. 81st St. ((C) **800/368-4575** or 212/362-9200; www.excelsiorhotelny.com). $$$ **Le Parker Meridien,** 119 W. 56th St. (pedestrian entrance: 118 W. 57th St.; (C) **800/543-4300** or 212/245-5000; www.parkermeridien.com).

WHY THEY'LL THANK YOU: One percent inspiration, 99% perspiration.

Hoover Dam
Concrete Colossus of the Southwest
Ages 6 & up • Boulder City, Nevada

U.S. 93, WHICH RUNS BETWEEN LAS VEGAS, NEVADA, AND KING-
man, Arizona, lays its ribbon of concrete right across one of the
great engineering wonders of the world, **Hoover Dam.** Built
between 1931 and 1935, this behemoth Depression-era project
redrew the map of America: If it hadn't been for Hoover Dam, Arizona and California would never have had enough electricity and
water to sustain their subsequent population boom. And yes, the
dam also created the largest artificial lake in the United States,
110-mile-long **Lake Mead.** Driving across Hoover Dam, traffic
crawls as motorists gape at the view, with smooth Lake Mead on
one hand and a plummeting gorge on the other. But why let the
kids be content with a mere view, when you can go inside the belly
of the beast?

Going face to face with this much concrete is an awesome experience. Hoover Dam stands 726 feet tall from bedrock to the road-
way atop it. At the top, it's 45 feet thick, which is stout enough, but
it widens the farther down you go, until at the base it's a whopping
660 feet thick. The dam was named after Herbert Hoover, not just
because he was president when the bill was signed to build it, but
because the Boulder Canyon dam was in many ways his idea—as
Secretary of Commerce in the early 1920s, Hoover, a civil engineer
himself, first urged the southwestern states to consider such an
undertaking.

While much of the Hoover Dam story is told via **historic photographs** in interpretive galleries, the part kids really remember is
taking **elevators** 500 feet down into the wall of Black Canyon, and
then walking down a 250-foot-long tunnel to look at the guts of the
power plant, with its eight huge generators. At the end of the tour,
don't miss going up to the observation deck to get that **panoramic
view** of Lake Mead and the Colorado basin. Functional as it is in

many ways, the dam still has a streamlined Art Deco flair—check out the sculptured panels decorating the central two elevator towers rising from the top of the dam, the Nevada one celebrating the dam's benefits—flood control, navigation, irrigation, water supply, and power—the Arizona one paying tribute to Indian tribes that once lived here.

Hoover Dam makes a handy day trip from Las Vegas, 30 miles away, though I'd recommend combining a Hoover Dam visit with a stay on Lake Mead in a **houseboat** (contact **Seven Crown Resorts,** Box 16247, Irvine, CA; © **800/752-9669;** www.seven crown.com). Another fun way to visit the dam is on a **paddle-wheeler cruise** from **Lake Mead Cruises** (© **702/293-6180;** www.lakemeadcruises.com).

ⓘ U.S. 93 (© **866/730-9097** or 702/494-2517; www.usbr.gov/lc/hooverdam).

✈ Las Vegas McCarran International.

🛏 $$ **Mandalay Bay,** 3950 Las Vegas Blvd. S. (© **877/632-7800** or 702/632-7777; www.mandalaybay.com). $$ **MGM Grand,** 3799 Las Vegas Blvd. S. (© **877/880-0880** or 702/891-7777; www.mgmgrand.com).

WHY THEY'LL THANK YOU: Feeling the power of those generators.

Stargazing   58

Griffith Observatory
Planetarium Hollywood
Ages 6 & up • Los Angeles, California

FILM BUFFS INSTANTLY RECOGNIZE THIS STREAMLINED **ART DECO observatory** in L.A.'s rambling Griffith Park from the climactic scenes of the 1955 James Dean classic film *Rebel Without a Cause.*

My kids, however, know it from the climactic scenes of the 1999 Steve Martin/Eddie Murphy comedy *Bowfinger*. But so what if they don't get the *Rebel Without a Cause* reference? Who could fail to dig this white stucco complex with its three bronze domes, slung into the south side of Mount Hollywood with a killer panorama of Los Angeles spread out below? In the daytime, the lawn of the observatory is one of the best places in the city to view the famous Hollywood sign; on warm nights, with the lights twinkling below, the Griffith Observatory's wide terrace is one of the most romantic places in L.A. And if you manage to steer the children inside to do a little stargazing while you're up there at night, you're ahead of the game.

This Hollywood Hills landmark was built in 1935 in the vaguely Mediterranean style studio moguls of that era favored and underwent a major renovation during 2003–06. A white obelisk in front honors six great astronomers of the past: Hipparchus, Copernicus, Galileo, Kepler, Newton, and Herschel. The large central dome houses a state-of-the-art **planetarium,** where narrated projectors

The Griffith Observatory.

display the stars and planets that are nearly impossible to observe outdoors, what with all the smog and light pollution of the L.A. metro sprawl. Like most planetariums, it also screens various multimedia shows of varying scientific seriousness. We generally skip the planetarium, however, and head straight into the adjacent exhibits on galaxies, meteorites, and other astronomical subjects, which include cool objects such as a mechanical orrery, a Tesla coil, and scales where you can check your weight on different planets. A Foucault pendulum mesmerized my boys as it methodically swung in the main rotunda, demonstrating the earth's rotation, and detailed 6-foot topographical models of the earth and the moon provide focal points in the side galleries.

The observatory's two flanking domes each house a telescope—in the west one, a triple-beamed **solar telescope** trained on the sun for daytime visitors, in the east one a 12-inch **refracting telescope.** On clear nights visitors can climb to the roof and wait their turn to gaze through it at the moon and planets. This is, after all, an observatory, and although it has never had the astronomical prestige of its California neighbor **Palomar Mountain,** it does attend to sky matters.

(i) 2800 E. Observatory Rd., Los Angeles (© **213/473-0800;** www. griffithobs.org).

✈ Los Angeles International.

🛏 $$$ **The Beverly Garland Holiday Inn,** 4222 Vineland Ave., North Hollywood (© **800/BEVERLY** [238-3759] or 818/980-8000; www.beverlygarland.com). $$ **Hollywood Roosevelt Hotel,** 7000 Hollywood Blvd. (© **800/950-7667** or 323/466-7000; www. hollywoodroosevelt.com).

WHY THEY'LL THANK YOU: A chance to study the other Hollywood stars.

Mauna Kea
Stargazing at the Top of the World

Ages 12 & up (summit), 10 & up (visitor center) •
Mauna Kea, Hawaii

THE SNOWCAPPED SUMMIT OF MAUNA KEA—THE WORLD'S TALLEST mountain, if measured from its base on the ocean floor—is the best place on earth for astronomical observation. It's not just the height, it's also its location near the equator, where clear, pollution-free skies give way to pitch-black nights undisturbed by urban light. That's why Mauna Kea is home to no fewer than 13 world-class telescopes, including the **Keck Telescopes,** among the world's largest. Even with the naked eye, the stargazing from here is fantastic.

Many tours that go to the summit won't take anyone under 16 or any pregnant women, due to the high altitude. If you opt not to go up, it's still cool to view the model of the Keck Telescope down in Waimea, 65-1120 Mamalahoa Hwy. (© 808/885-7887; www.keckobservatory.org). Developed by the University of California and the California Institute of Technology, the Keck is an infrared telescope eight stories high, weighing 150 tons, and with a 33-foot-diameter mirror made of 36 perfectly attuned hexagon mirrors—like a fly's eye—rather than one conventional lens.

You'll need a four-wheel-drive vehicle if you do drive up the mountain. The **Visitor Information Station** at the **Onizuka Center,** named after a Hawaiian astronaut who died in the *Challenger* explosion, is an hour's drive from Hilo or Waimea; from Hwy. 190, take the narrow, rutted Saddle Road (Hwy. 200) 28 miles, then turn onto unmarked Summit Road, and go another 6¼ miles to the Visitor Information Station. At this point you're already 9,000 feet up, so stop for half an hour to acclimate. With younger kids, this may be your endpoint, so time your visit to join the nighttime **stargazing sessions,** 6 to 10pm, which include a lecture, a video, and the chance to peer through 11-inch, 14-inch, and 16-inch telescopes.

The Keck Telescopes at Mauna Kea.

It's 6 miles from here to the summit, but it can take 45 minutes to drive this rough, unpaved, winding road, in low gear all the way—a climb of another 4,200 feet—to 13,796-foot-high **Observatory Hill.** Dress warmly and drink lots of liquid; wear dark glasses to avoid snow blindness; and use plenty of sunscreen. At the top, 11 nations, including the U.S., Japan, the U.K., France, and Australia, have set up 13 powerful infrared telescopes to look into deep space. Visitors can't use those telescopes, of course, though you can look at a couple (including the Keck) from galleries. If you take a narrow foot-path past the observatories, there's a cairn of rocks where you can sit and contemplate an incredible 360-degree view across the Pacific. Even if you're socked in by clouds, it's a true top-of-the-world view, with the summits of Mauna Loa and Maui's Haleakala poking through the puffy white cumulus clouds beneath your feet.

ⓘ ✆ **808/961-2180;** www.ifa.hawaii.edu/info/vis.

✈ Hilo International, 29 miles.

🛏 $$ **Kilauea Lodge,** Old Volcano Rd., off Hwy. 11 (✆ **808/967-7366;** www.kilauealodge.com).

WHY THEY'LL THANK YOU: That monster telescope, that killer view.

The Cable Car Hills of San Francisco

All ages • San Francisco, California

MAYBE IT WAS ALL THOSE RICE-A-RONI® COMMERCIALS FROM MY childhood, but I get a thrill when I hear the clang-clang of a **San Francisco cable car.** These beloved wooden icons, the only moving landmarks in the National Register of Historic Places, are absurdly impractical; San Francisco had nearly torn up all the tracks in 1947 until a public outcry saved the last three lines. And now, whaddya know, they are San Francisco's most iconic attraction, the one must-do for every visitor.

A San Francisco cable car.

San Francisco's steep hills are notorious; it's a great location for filming car chases (remember *Bullitt*?) but a challenging place for everyone else. In 1869 engineer Andrew Hallidie watched a team of overworked horses pulling a heavy carriage up a rain-slicked San Francisco hill and resolved to invent a mechanical device to replace the beasts; in 1873 the first cable car traversed Clay Street. They really are ingenious: An electrically powered steel cable under the street constantly moves at 9½ mph, which each car clamps onto with an underground grip to get hauled along (operators are thus called "grippers," not drivers). Listen for the distinctive underground click-ity-clack of the cable. Daredevils choose to ride in the open-air sections, not the enclosed seating areas, standing up and hanging onto a strap, which at under 10 mph isn't as perilous as it sounds.

Two cable car routes start at the intersection of Powell and Market streets: The **Powell-Hyde line** ends at the turnaround in a waterfront park by Ghirardelli Square, and the **Powell-Mason line** meanders through North Beach to end on the east side of Fisherman's Wharf. The Powell-Hyde line has the steepest climbs and drops, if that's what you're interested in; take it from Market Street north, past crooked Lombard Street on your right, before heading down Russian Hill with a breathtaking vista of Alcatraz ⑭ and the San Francisco Bay. The **California Street line** runs east–west from Market and California streets over Nob Hill to Van Ness Avenue. Queues to board the Powell Street cars at either end seem endless, but there are strategies to avoid them: Ride at less-popular night hours, jump on at an intermediate stop (this is iffy in high season, when cars get so full that they can't pick up passengers en route), or board at Powell and Market rather than the crowded turnarounds near Fisherman's Wharf (for the California line, the Van Ness end is less crowded). Even though we waited for over an hour at the Ghirardelli Square terminus, we actually had fun—street musicians played, tourists swapped travel tips, and we could watch three or four cars pivot grandly around on the turntables. After that long wait, the ride seemed surprisingly short, but no one in my family complained.

ⓘ **SF Cable Car** (www.sfcablecar.com). **San Francisco Municipal Transportation Agency** (www.sfmta.com). **San Francisco Travel Association,** 900 Market St. (☏ 415/391-2000; www.sanfrancisco.travel).

✈ San Francisco International, 13 miles. Oakland International, 18 miles.

🛏 $$$ **Argonaut Hotel,** 495 Jefferson St. (℅ **866/415-0704** or 415/563-0800; www.argonauthotel.com). $$ **Larkspur Hotel,** 524 Sutter St. (℅ **866/823-4669** or 415/421-2865; www.larkspurhotel unionsquare.com).

WHY THEY'LL THANK YOU: The San Francisco treat.

Masterpieces of Art

The Metropolitan Museum of Art
Manhattan's Treasure Trove
All ages • New York, New York

THE ECHOING MARBLE-CLAD GREAT HALL TELLS YOU AS YOU ENTER that this is a Serious Art Museum. But don't let that put you off—New York City's number-one tourist attraction can be a lot of fun for children, even toddlers. Make a beeline for the areas kids really love: **Arms and Armor** (first floor), the extensive **Egyptian rooms** (also on the first floor—don't miss the glorious mummies), **musical instruments** (second floor, off the American Wing's courtyard), the **Costume Institute** (ground floor—rotating installations will often be of interest to kids), and the **European and American furniture rooms** (all over the place—any kid who's read *From the Mixed-Up Files of Mrs. Basil E. Frankweiler,* about a brother and sister who hide out for weeks in the Met, will adore these). On the first floor of the **American Wing,** a side gallery displays vintage baseball cards, and a whole gallery of grandfather clocks ticks away on the second floor. Older kids who are beginning to appreciate art may go for the **Impressionist gallery** (second floor), full of Monets and van Goghs they'll instantly recognize, or the **Lehman Wing,** set up like the town house of the wealthy collector—it's art in small enough doses that it doesn't overwhelm.

Main stairway at the Metropolitan Museum of Art.

Our favorite corner, hands down, is the **courtyard of the American Wing,** a light-filled open space with plantings, benches, and statues kids can actually relate to (a mountain lion and her cubs, a pensive Indian brave). Back in the corner is an entire Frank Lloyd Wright room—all dark wood and low-slung right angles—that our family could move into at a moment's notice. Bring lots of small change for kids to throw into the American Wing reflecting pool and in the pool in front of the Egyptian Wing's serene **Temple of Dendur.** In the Japanese galleries, find the room overlooking the Temple of Dendur; off the musical instruments gallery, find the balcony overlooking the mounted knights in armor.

The huge museum gift shop has a lot of good stuff for kids, and there are plenty of free children's programs.

(i) 1000 Fifth Ave., at 82nd St. ((C) **212/535-7710;** www.met museum.org).

✈ John F. Kennedy International, Newark Liberty International, LaGuardia.

🛏 $$ **Excelsior Hotel,** 45 W. 81st St. (✆ **800/368-4575** or 212/362-9200; www.excelsiorhotelny.com). $$$ **Le Parker Meridien,** 119 W. 56th St. (pedestrian entrance: 118 W. 57th St.; ✆ **800/543-4300** or 212/245-5000; www.parkermeridien.com).

WHY THEY'LL THANK YOU: Great art is great art.

The Art Institute of Chicago
Hitting Art's Highlights in the Loop
Ages 4 & up • Chicago, Illinois

MY KIDS ARE GREAT FANS OF THE MOVIE *FERRIS BUELLER'S DAY OFF,* the greatest Chicago travelogue ever made, in my opinion. What Ferris (Matthew Broderick) and his two pals do in Chicago while playing hooky from their nice North Shore high school is our dream itinerary for a day in the Windy City: a Cubs game, a parade—and a stroll through the Art Institute of Chicago. If it was fun enough for Ferris, my kids figured, it would be fun enough for them.

Of course we were compelled to begin, like Ferris, with the immense pointillist canvas by Georges Seurat, **Sunday Afternoon on the Island of La Grande Jatte.** Like every other visitor there, we alternated standing up close to see the individual dots and then standing way back until the dots blur into a busy panorama of springtime in the park. After *La Grande Jatte,* we wandered dreamily through the rest of the **Impressionists,** a collection so rich in Renoirs and Monets that we almost felt a sugar high; we hunted down the van Gogh self-portrait and then Picasso's blue-period *The Old Guitarist* and felt very satisfied.

Going from the hazy Impressionists to sharply detailed 20th-century American paintings was a bracing contrast. We homed in on two masterpieces: the iconic **American Gothic,** by Grant Wood, which they've seen spoofed so often, and Edward Hopper's evocative late-night diner scene **Nighthawks.** Then off we went to my favorite nook in the museum: the reconstructed turn-of-the-century **Chicago Stock Exchange Trading Room,** a dazzling Louis Sullivan showpiece with art-glass insets and stenciled decorations and molded plaster capitals—a perfect expression of Gilded Age tycoonery.

From there, we zigzagged back to the **Thorne Miniature Rooms,** filled with tiny reproductions of furnished interiors from European and American history (heaven for my dollhouse-loving daughter), and then rewarded the boys for their patience with a browse through the great hall of **European arms and armor,** where more than 1,500 objects range from horse armor to maces to poleaxes.

We missed the world-famous collection of glass paperweights; we missed the splendid Japanese wood block prints—who cared? We didn't even worry about plotting a logical course through the museum, since scuttling back and forth allowed us to pass Marc Chagall's jewel-toned **stained-glass windows** more than once, always a good thing.

(i) 111 S. Michigan Ave. (© **312/443-3600;** www.artic.edu).

✈ O'Hare International, 15 miles. Midway International, 12 miles.

🛏 $$ **Homewood Suites by Hilton,** 40 E. Grand Ave. (© **800/ CALL-HOME** [225-5466] or 312/644-2222; www.homewoodsuites chicago.com). $$ **Hotel Allegro Chicago,** 171 W. Randolph St. (© **800/643-1500** or 312/236-0123; www.allegrochicago.com).

WHY THEY'LL THANK YOU: Connecting the dots.

Huntington Library
Pasadena's Great Portrait Gallery
Ages 6 & up • San Marino, California

THE WORD "LIBRARY" IN THE NAME MAY MAKE THE KIDS WINCE—WHY visit a musty old library on vacation? Well, even if they wanted to, they couldn't flip through the rare items in Henry E. Huntington's book collection. What they can see, though, is his terrific art collection in a stately Italianate mansion on a 207-acre hilltop estate.

As a girl, I was captivated by one pair of paintings here: Thomas Gainsborough's **The Blue Boy** and Thomas Lawrence's **Pinkie**, a long-haired boy in blue satin and a slim, dark-haired girl in a filmy white gown and pink bonnet, warily eyeing each other from facing walls of a wood-paneled salon. These life-size paintings capture the moodiness of adolescence so perfectly, you almost expect the kids to step out of those frames and start dissing each other. Blue Boy—aka Jonathan Buttall, son of a wealthy hardware merchant—peers guardedly at us, left hand cockily set on his hip. Pinkie—in real life Sarah Barrett Moulton, an aunt to the Victorian poet Elizabeth Barrett Browning—stands poised on tiptoe, the satin ribbons of her askew bonnet fluttering, one hand raised defensively. Stormy skies boil behind both

The Japanese Garden at Huntington Library.

119

subjects, mirroring their defiant teenage expressions. *Pinkie* was painted 25 years after *Blue Boy,* and there was no specific connection between the two—until Henry Huntington bought them both and set them here, a sort of blind date for eternity.

It's always interesting to see great art in a private home setting (if nothing else, it's less intimidating for children than a big formal art museum), but it's particularly apt for 18th-century **English portraits,** which were originally commissioned by aristocrats to decorate their own country manors. The Huntington's main gallery presents the best assemblage anywhere of **full-figure English portraits,** with work by Romney and Reynolds as well as Gainsborough and Lawrence—the Fab Four of late-18th-century portraiture. And the Huntington adds the final touch by serving daily **high tea** (or at any rate what Americans think of as high tea, with pastries and finger sandwiches) in a tearoom overlooking a fabulous rose garden. (Call ✆ **626/683-8131** for reservations, at least 2 weeks in advance.) For locals, the **botanical gardens** are the Huntington's main draw—an exotic cactus garden, a lush jungle garden, soothing lily ponds, and a Japanese garden with open-air house, koi-filled stream, and Zen garden. The gardens are lovely indeed, though Blue Boy and Pinkie are what make us return.

ⓘ 1151 Oxford Rd. (✆ **626/405-2100;** www.huntington.org).

✈ Los Angeles International.

🛏 $$$ **The Beverly Garland Holiday Inn,** 4222 Vineland Ave., North Hollywood (✆ **800/BEVERLY** [238-3759] or 818/980-8000; www.beverlygarland.com). $$ **Hollywood Roosevelt Hotel,** 7000 Hollywood Blvd. (✆ **800/950-7667** or 323/466-7000; www.hollywoodroosevelt.com).

WHY THEY'LL THANK YOU: Blue Boy and Pinkie, sitting in a tree . . .

Graceland
Memphis Music Mecca
Ages 6 & up • Memphis, Tennessee

TO MANY MUSIC FANS, MEMPHIS, TENNESSEE, MEANS ONE THING: the world's greatest Elvis shrine, Graceland. But chances are your kids know more about tacky Elvis impersonators than they do about the King himself. So when you come to Memphis, show them the whole story—the amazing music heritage that first drew the shy teenager from Tupelo, Mississippi, to this Tennessee river city. Begin on **Beale Street,** the nerve center of the South's most vital post–Civil War black community. W. C. Handy brought the blues sound up Hwy. 61 from Mississippi at the turn of the century and it caught fire in the clubs of Beale Street; later, such legends as B. B. King, Muddy Waters, and Howlin' Wolf added their voices. Stroll along the street, read the historic markers, and check out who's playing at the nightclubs between Second and Fourth streets. Visit the **W. C. Handy House Museum,** 352 Beale St. (✆ **901/527-3427**), and the Smithsonian's **Memphis Rock 'n' Soul Museum,** 191 Beale St. (✆ **901/205-2533;** www.memphisrocknsoul.org), with photos, recordings, and artifacts, from a satin Elvis Presley suit to Ike Turner's piano.

In 1950, in a tiny brick corner storefront, recording engineer Sam Phillips opened **Sun Studio,** 706 Union Ave. (✆ **800/441-6249** or 901/521-0664; www.sunstudio.com), where then-unknowns Carl Perkins, Roy Orbison, Jerry Lee Lewis, Johnny Cash, and Elvis Presley took the blues sound, mixed it with country and bluegrass, and came up with a new sound: rock 'n' roll. You can tour Sun Studio's surprisingly Spartan setup; records are still made here by such current artists as U2 and Bonnie Raitt.

Yet another sound was born in Memphis in 1959, when Stax Records began recording such soul-music greats as Isaac Hayes, Otis Redding, and Wilson Pickett. The **Stax Museum of American Soul Music,** 926 E. McLemore Ave. (✆ **901/942-SOUL** [942-7685]

121

or 901/946-2535; www.staxmuseum.com), has such evocative exhibits as a re-created gospel church and the dance floor from the TV show *Soul Train.*

Now that you've placed Elvis in music history, head out on Elvis Presley Boulevard to **Graceland,** the colonial-style mansion Elvis bought in the late 1950s for the then-huge price of $100,000. As the King's fame grew, 14-acre Graceland became his refuge, and eventually his retreat from reality. Touring the mansion, you'll get a glimpse of the lavish lifestyle the poor Delta boy chose once he hit the big time: carpeted wall-to-wall in white, with gold accents and satin drapes everywhere. Walls covered with gold record plaques, mannequin after mannequin sporting Elvis's stage outfits—it's an assault on the senses. Don't miss the flower-laden memorial garden where Elvis is buried alongside his parents. It completes the whole arc of Elvis's career, from raw young rockabilly to hip-swiveling teen heartthrob to sequin-jumpsuited megastar. As you drive away, play a mix-tape of Elvis hits from "That's All Right, Mama" and "All Shook Up" to "Love Me Tender" and "Suspicious Minds." Now the kids know who Elvis is.

ⓘ 3734 Elvis Presley Blvd. (✆ **800/238-2000** or 901/332-3322; www.elvis.com).

✈ Memphis International.

🛏 $$ **Homewood Suites by Hilton,** 5811 Poplar Ave. (✆ **800/ CALL-HOME** [225-5466] or 901/763-0500; www.homewoodsuites. com). $$$ **The Peabody Memphis,** 149 Union Ave. (✆ **800/PEA-BODY** [732-2639] or 901/529-4000; www.peabodymemphis.com).

WHY THEY'LL THANK YOU: Elvis never left *this* building.

65 **Music**

The Nashville Music Scene
Country Music's Capital
Ages 8 & up • Nashville, Tennessee

NASHVILLE: THE VERY NAME IS SYNONYMOUS WITH MUSIC, SPECIFICALLY the brand of country music played on the Grand Ole Opry radio show, broadcast from here since 1927. To perform on the Grand Ole Opry is to officially "make it" in country music, and thus it's a town buzzing with music-biz execs, state-of-the-art studios, and happening clubs, with a surprising amount of jazz and rock going down as well. I love Nashville, and even though I'm no country-music aficionado, it only takes a couple hours here to get hooked on its twangy energy.

A music pilgrimage to Nashville centers on three areas: down-town near Ryman Auditorium, the original home of the Opry; in the West End along 16th Avenue, known as Music Row, where you can often spot music stars going in and out of the studios; and east of town at the vast Opryland complex where the Opry relocated in 1974. Out at Opryland, the current **Grand Ole Opry House,** 2802 Opryland Dr. (© **800/SEE-OPRY** [733-6779] or 615/871-6779; www.opry.com), produces three live TV shows a week, April to December—order your tickets well in advance. Exhibits at the **Grand Ole Opry Museum** next door celebrate Opry stars past and present. For a more rounded idea of country music, though, head downtown for the **Country Music Hall of Fame and Museum,** 222 Fifth Ave. S. (© **800/852-6437** or 615/416-2001; www.countrymusichalloffame.com). From sequin-spangled cos-tumes to historic guitars to over-the-top custom cars (a crucial status symbol in country music culture), it's an impressive roundup of artifacts, and the kids really get into the video and audio clips, interactive jukeboxes, and touch-screen computer kiosks, explor-ing the differences between intertwined musical genres—blue-grass, cowboy music, rockabilly, Cajun, honky-tonk, country swing. Once you're grounded in the music, walk 2 blocks to the **Ryman**

Auditorium, 116 Fifth Ave. N. (✆ **615/889-3060;** www.ryman.com), aka The Mother Church of Country Music (built as a church in 1892, it still has stained-glass windows). Dowdy as it looks outside, inside it's a finely restored arena-like theater with top acoustics. By day, it offers memorabilia exhibits, a backstage dressing room tour, and a booth where you can record your own live CD; by night, it has a full roster of live concerts. Then take in an early-evening show at the **Bluebird Café,** 4104 Hillsboro Pike (✆ **615/383-1461;** www.bluebirdcafe.com), to hear today's up-and-coming singer-songwriters.

ⓘ **Nashville Visitor Information Center,** Bridgestone Arena, 501 Broadway, at Fifth Ave. S. (✆ **800/657-6910** or 615/259-4747; www.visitmusiccity.com).

✈ Nashville International, 8 miles.

🛏 $$ **Courtyard by Marriott Nashville Vanderbilt/West End,** 1901 West End Ave. (✆ **800/245-1959** or 615/327-9900; www.marriott.com/bnawe). $$–$$$ **Gaylord Opryland,** 2800 Opryland Dr. (✆ **866/972-6779** or 615/889-1000; www.gaylordhotels.com/gaylord-opryland).

WHY THEY'LL THANK YOU: When their boots start a-tapping.

Rock and Roll Hall of Fame
Cleveland Rocks
Ages 6 & up • Cleveland, Ohio

WHY CLEVELAND? WHY NOT? THIS IS THE TOWN WHERE DJ ALAN Freed first coined the term *rock 'n' roll*, where Chuck Berry played his first public gig; it's the hometown of musicians from Phil Ochs to Chrissie Hynde to Trent Reznor. And what's more, it's within a day's drive of 50% of the U.S. population, so this high-profile shrine can be visited by as many music lovers as possible.

Designed by I. M. Pei, the museum building is an all-shook-up mass of porcelain-tiled geometric shapes, piled up like a guitar and

The Rock and Roll Hall of Fame.

amps in the back of a roadie's van, with a glass pyramid jutting out from one side over Lake Erie. Inside is a cool collection of **pop-culture memorabilia** to browse through. Even if you and the kids don't listen to the same artists, there's plenty here for everyone to groove on. Exhibits display programs, posters, photos, instruments (from Junior Walker's lovingly shined saxophone to a smashed guitar from Paul Simonon of the Clash), and stage costumes (James Brown's red rhinestone-studded tuxedo coat, Neil Young's fringed leather jacket). But what really grabs kids are the artifacts from rock stars' childhoods—things like Jimi Hendrix's baby picture, Jim Morrison's Cub Scout uniform, John Lennon's report card, Joe Walsh's high-school football jersey. Not to ignore current chart toppers, on the plaza level a rotating exhibit features today's artists, from Phantom Planet to the Jonas Brothers. For those of us who actually remember the 1950s, the **Rave On exhibit** displays mementos from such rock 'n' rollers as Eddie Cochran, Buddy Holly, and the Everly Brothers on a curved wall evoking a chrome-and-neon diner.

Still, rock 'n' roll isn't about artifacts, it's about performance. Up in the **Hall of Fame,** a video collage of all the 200-plus inductees is mesmerizing. The Hall of Fame includes mostly musicians (eligible 25 years after their first record release), as well as a few producers, DJs, and journalists. Though displays near the entrance focus on the most recent class of inductees, huge "virtual jukebox" stations let you access just about any song recorded by any Hall of Famer; their autographs are etched in glass on a great wall projecting over the lake. As with all such ventures, the list of who's in and who's not is controversial, but then that makes for great dinner-table arguments.

(i) 1100 Rock and Roll Blvd., at E. 9th St. (© **888/764-ROCK** [7625] or 216/781-7625; www.rockhall.com).

✈ Cleveland Hopkins International, 10 miles.

⊨ $$ **Cleveland Marriott Downtown at Key Center,** 127 Public Sq. (© **888/236-2427** or 216/696-9200; www.marriott.com). $$ **DoubleTree by Hilton Cleveland Downtown/Lakeside,** 1111 Lakeside Ave. (© **800/222-TREE** [222-8733] or 216/241-5100; www.doubletree.com).

WHY THEY'LL THANK YOU: It's only rock 'n' roll, but they'll like it.

67 The Movies

Hooray for Hollywood
Movie Mecca
Ages 8 & up • Hollywood, California

THE NAME HOLLYWOOD MAY BE SYNONYMOUS WITH MOVIEMAKING, BUT many tourists are disappointed by how shabby the town itself is. I relish its seedy, down-at-the-heels aura, but my kids were not impressed—until they got an eyeful of **Grauman's Chinese Theatre,** 6925 Hollywood Blvd. ((© 323/464-MANN [6266]; www.chinese theatres.com), still one of the world's great movie palaces, with over-the-top Chinese embellishments and an entry court where such stars as Elizabeth Taylor have set their signatures and hand-and footprints in cement. So what if the kids didn't recognize most of the names? Nearby is the relatively recently built **Kodak Theatre,** 6801 Hollywood Blvd., where they give out the Oscars every year; we also marveled at the refurbished **Egyptian Theatre,** 6712 Hollywood Blvd., and the Art Deco **Pantages Theatre,** 6233 Hollywood Blvd., for a *Sunset Boulevard* taste of 1920s glamour. Stars who couldn't get a spot at Grauman's were honored with bronze medallions in the pavement along the **Hollywood Walk of Fame,** Hollywood Boulevard between Gower Street and La Brea Avenue; and Vine Street, between Yucca Street and Sunset Boulevard (© 323/469-8311; www.hollywoodchamber.net). John Lennon, Elvis Presley, and Eddie Murphy, those were medallions worth a snapshot or two.

But why settle for sidewalk plaques when you can see films really being made? A quick prefab version is the hour-long tram tour at **Universal Studios Hollywood,** Hollywood Freeway (CA 170), Universal Center Drive or Lankershim Boulevard exits, Universal City (© 800/UNIVERSAL [864-8377]; www.universalstudios hollywood.com); but these days, thrill rides are more Universal's raison d'être. We'd rather walk around the wardrobe and prop departments, back lots, and active sets of a real working studio. These walking tours run Monday through Friday and last 2 hours or

The emblematic Hollywood sign in the Hollywood Hills of Los Angeles.

more; advance reservations are essential. Here are your options: **Paramount Pictures,** 5555 Melrose Ave. (© **323/956-1777;** www.paramountstudios.com; ages 12 and up); **Warner Brothers Studios,** 3400 Riverside Dr., Burbank (© **877/492-8687;** www. wbstudiotour.com; ages 9 and up); **Sony Pictures,** 10202 W. Washington Blvd., Culver City (© **310/244-TOUR** [8687]; www. sonypicturesstudios.com; ages 12 and up); and **NBC Studios,** 3000 W. Alameda Ave., Burbank (© **818/840-3537;** www.studio audiences.com).

Or you can get free tickets to join the studio audience for a sitcom or talk show taping (however, many shows don't admit children under the age of 10 or even 18). For these, contact well in advance: **Audiences Unlimited, Inc.** (© **818/260-0041;** www.tvtickets. com); **TVTIX.COM** (© **818/985-8811;** www.tvtix.com); **CBS Television City** (© **323/575-2458**); **NBC Studios** (© **818/840-3537**); **Paramount Studios** (© **323/956-1777;** www.paramountstudios. com); or **Universal Studios** (© **800/UNIVERSAL** [864-8377]; www. universalstudios.com).

ⓘ **Hollywood Visitor Information Center,** 6801 Hollywood Blvd. (℃ **323/467-6412;** www.discoverlosangeles.com).

✈ Los Angeles International.

🛏 $$$ **The Beverly Garland Holiday Inn,** 4222 Vineland Ave., North Hollywood (℃ **800/BEVERLY** [238-3759] or 818/980-8000; www.beverlygarland.com). $$ **Hollywood Roosevelt Hotel,** 7000 Hollywood Blvd. (℃ **800/950-7667** or 323/466-7000; www. hollywoodroosevelt.com).

WHY THEY'LL THANK YOU: Seeing stars.

68 Castles & Mansions

Newport's Mansions
The Gilded Age Elite's Summer "Cottages"

Ages 8 & up • Newport, Rhode Island

Driving around Newport, Rhode Island, you can't help but gawp at the turn-of-the-20th-century mansions—Italianate *palazzi,* Tudor-style manors, faux French château, all set in elegant formal landscaping, with imposing gates or walls to keep out hoi polloi (for example, *you*). It's incredible to imagine the sort of wealth that built these homes, even more incredible to realize that these were just these families' summer houses (offhandedly referred to as mere "cottages").

While many of these houses are still private property, nine are open to the public for guided tours, popular with tourists year-round (though not all are open daily in winter). Don't cram too many into 1 day—the sheer opulence of these interiors can soon bring on sensory overload. The most popular is **The Breakers,** 44 Ochre Point Ave. (℃ **401/847-1000**), a 70-room 1895 mansion designed for Commodore Vanderbilt by Richard Morris Hunt. Patterned after Renaissance Florentine *palazzi,* it has a stunning great hall, an ornate 50-foot cube sheathed in marble. The Breakers even

The Breakers in Newport.

has bathrooms (very high-tech for the time) where both fresh and salt water come out of the taps. Stanford White modeled **Rosecliff,** 548 Bellevue Ave. (© **401/847-1000**), after the Grand Trianon at Versailles. Built in 1902 for an heiress of the Comstock Lode mining fortune, it has only 40 rooms (how sad), but it also has Newport's largest ballroom and a heart-shaped grand staircase.

Two other Bellevue Avenue houses belonged to the same woman—named Alva Vanderbilt when she was mistress of **Marble House,** 596 Bellevue Ave. (© **401/847-1000**), so called because it shows off just about every type of marble there is. Its ballroom is literally dazzling, with three kinds of gold encrusting its walls. Alva divorced her Vanderbilt husband and promptly married his best friend, who was a Belmont and lived down the street at **Belcourt Castle,** 657 Bellevue Ave. (© **401/846-0669;** www.belcourtcastle. com). My daughter couldn't get over the luxurious stables. The Breakers may have had bathrooms, but Belcourt Castle had electricity, designed by Thomas Edison, no less. Tell the kids to look for the 14 secret doors.

(i) **Preservation Society of Newport,** 424 Bellevue Ave. (© **401/847-1000;** www.newportmansions.org).

✈ Providence T. F. Green International, 28 miles.

🛏 $$$ **Hyatt Regency Newport,** 1 Goat Island (© **800/233-1234** or 401/851-1234; www.hyatt.com). $$ **Mill Street Inn,** 75 Mill St. (© **800/392-1316** or 401/849-9500; www.millstreetinn. com).

BEST TIME: December, when the houses are decorated for the holidays.

WHY THEY'LL THANK YOU: Imagine sliding down these banisters.

Castles & Mansions

Hearst Castle
California Palace in the Sky
Ages 8 & up • San Simeon, California

IT'S NOT ENTIRELY TRUE THAT THE HILLTOP CALIFORNIA ESTATE OF publishing magnate William Randolph Hearst is a 20th-century replica of an Old World manor. True, it was built from 1919 to 1947, but the bits and pieces are nearly all authentic—400-year-old Spanish and Italian ceilings, 500-year-old mantels, 16th-century Florentine bedsteads, Renaissance paintings, Flemish tapestries, and innumerable other European treasures, which Hearst compulsively acquired for years.

Each week, railroad cars carrying fragments of Roman temples, carved doors from Italian monasteries, hastily rolled canvases by the old masters, ancient Persian rugs, and antique French furniture arrived—5 tons at a time—in San Simeon. Orson Welles's 1941 masterpiece *Citizen Kane,* a thinly disguised fictional biography of Hearst, has an unforgettable shot of priceless antiques warehoused in dusty piles, stretching as far as the eye can see. Only a fraction of what Hearst bought was ever installed in the estate.

The Reflecting Pool at Hearst Castle.

Despite this patchwork approach, this sprawling Mediterranean Revival–style compound has a unified look, no doubt because one architect (and a woman at that, Julia Morgan) directed its entire 28-year creation. The main house alone, **Casa Grande,** has more than 100 rooms of baronial splendor. My kids lusted after the red-velvet-padded private movie theater where Hearst (also a movie mogul) screened first-run films. They longed to jump into the fabulous swimming pools—a Roman-inspired indoor pool with intricate mosaics, and the breathtaking outdoor Greco-Roman Neptune pool, flanked by marble colonnades that frame the distant sea.

Book your **guided tour** in advance if possible—there's not much else around this stretch of California coast, so Hearst Castle doesn't cater to drop-in business (everybody staying at our motel either had been there that day or was going tomorrow). You'll park down at the visitor center and take a bus uphill to the compound. Three different daytime tours visit various parts of the estate, with very little overlap; they last about 2 hours. The **Grand Rooms Tour** covered all the essentials my kids wanted, but I regretted not seeing Hearst's private library and Gothic bedroom, which were on the **Upstairs Suites Tour.** There's also a **Cottages & Kitchen Tour.** Too bad the **Evening Tour** was full when we booked—for those, costumed docents portray Hearst's celebrity house party guests. Thanks to Hearst's mistress, actress Marion Davies, the estate was a playground for the Hollywood crowd.

(i) 750 Hearst Castle Rd. (CA 1; (✆ **805/927-2020,** or 800/444-4445 for tour reservations; www.hearstcastle.org).

✈ San Luis Obispo County Regional, 45 miles. Monterey Peninsula, 94 miles.

⌷ $$ **Best Western Cavalier Oceanfront Resort,** 9415 Hearst Dr. ((✆ **800/826-8168** or 805/927-4688; www.cavalier resort.com).

WHY THEY'LL THANK YOU: Versailles-scale opulence for an American Sun King.

70 **Famous Homesteads**

Orchard House
The Little Women *House*
Ages 6 & up • Concord, Massachusetts

EVEN GIRLS WHO HAVEN'T READ LOUISA MAY ALCOTT'S 1868 CLASSIC novel *Little Women* know the story from its many film versions and the Broadway musical. The story of its author, Louisa May Alcott—Jo in the novel—is even more powerful when you consider that she was one of the first women to earn a living as a writer. My daughter and I were thrilled to feel her presence hovering in every room of **Orchard House.**

The Alcott family lived from 1858 to 1877 in this saltbox-style frame house. Not only was *Little Women* set here, but it also was written here by the adult Louisa, at a shelf desk her father built between two windows in her bedroom. Although Louisa was 26 when they moved into Orchard House, she modeled the March family's house on it. Other family members were the models for the characters in *Little Women*: Anna ("Meg"), the eldest, an amateur actress; Elizabeth ("Beth"), a gifted musician who died before the family moved to this house; and May ("Amy"), a talented artist who went to study in Europe on Louisa's profits from *Little Women*. Their mother, the social activist Abigail May Alcott, frequently assumed the role of family breadwinner—her father, Louisa wrote in her journal, had "no gift for money making." Louisa herself, who never married, also helped support the family when she began to publish her short stories at age 22.

Visitors are guided through the modestly furnished house, which features many authentic heirlooms—the family china is laid out on the dining room table, props and costumes await their amateur theatricals, half-finished needleworks lie on side tables, and some of May's drawings are still scribbled on her bedroom walls. Anna's wedding was held in the parlor here, just as Meg's was, and all the sisters took turns cooking in the spartan kitchen.

Also in Concord is **The Wayside,** 455 Lexington Rd. (Ⓒ **978/318-7863;** www.nps.gov/mima; Wed–Sun late May to Oct only), the Alcotts' prior home (the girls called it "the yellow house"), where Nathaniel Hawthorne later lived, from 1852 until his death in 1864.

Ⓘ 399 Lexington Rd. (Ⓒ **978/369-4118;** www.louisamayalcott. org).

✈ Boston Logan International, 18 miles.

🛏 $$ **DoubleTree Suites by Hilton,** 400 Soldiers Field Rd. (Ⓒ **800/222-TREE** [8733] or 617/783-0090; www.doubletree.com). $ **The Midtown Hotel,** 220 Huntington Ave. (Ⓒ **800/343-1177** or 617/262-1000; www.midtownhotel.com).

WHY THEY'LL THANK YOU: Meg, Jo, Beth, and Amy live on here.

71

The Mark Twain Home
Tom Sawyer's Stomping Grounds
Ages 6 & up • Hannibal, Missouri

WHEN YOU ROLL INTO THIS LAID-BACK RIVER TOWN, ABOUT 130 MILES up the scenic Mississippi river road from St. Louis, you may get a nagging feeling that you've been here before. Well, you have—if you've read *The Adventures of Tom Sawyer*. Every scene in that book was based on affectionate memories of the town where a boy named Sam Clemens grew up, long before he became Mark Twain. Sometimes Hannibal leans on the association a bit too much— every third restaurant or shop seems to be named after a Tom Sawyer character—but the historic heart of town really does have a remarkable connection to this beloved American writer.

Eight properties around town, packaged under the name the Mark Twain Museum, have rock-solid associations with Sam Clemens. The main one is the small white frame house at 208 Hill St., where the Clemens family lived from 1844 to 1853; the parlor, the dining room, the kitchen, and the three upstairs bedrooms are all furnished in the period. You can almost imagine Sam climbing out the window of the back bedroom he shared with his brother Henry, sneaking off to nighttime escapades. Across the street is the much more prosperous house of the Hawkins family, whose daughter Laura—Twain's lifelong friend—was the model for Becky Thatcher. The law office of Sam's father, John Clemens, has been moved to the same street; its tiny front courtroom was the setting for Muff Potter's trial in *Tom Sawyer*. After a shift in the family fortunes, the Clemenses moved to cramped quarters above the old-fashioned pharmacy run by Dr. Orville Grant, over on Main Street. The last stop on this historic trail may not be authentic, but it could be the kids' favorite: the **Museum Gallery,** set in an old department store on Main Street, where interactive displays on *Tom Sawyer* allow children to whitewash a fence, hide in a spooky graveyard, and get lost in a cave, just like Tom and Huck and Becky did.

Of all the peripheral attractions in town, the one that has the most true Tom-'n'-Huck flavor is the **Mark Twain Cave,** 300 Cave Hollow Rd. (✆ **573/221-1656;** www.marktwaincave.com), a mile south of town on MO 79. Whether or not Sam Clemens actually got lost during a school picnic in either of these two caves, it's easy to imagine him making mischief down here, and the guides on the 1-hour tour are sure to work in references to the book.

Sleepy as Hannibal seems most of the year, it crackles to life during the **National Tom Sawyer Days** (www.hannibaljaycees.org/NTSD.html), the long weekend around July 4. All sorts of Twain-themed activities are held outdoors, from fence painting to frog jumping, and it's just generally the sort of whoop-de-do that Sam Clemens—or Tom Sawyer—would have loved.

ⓘ Mark Twain Boyhood Home & Museum, 120 N. Main St. (✆ **573/221-9010;** www.marktwainmuseum.org).

✈ Lambert–St. Louis International, 125 miles.

🛏 $$ **Best Western Plus on the River,** 401 N. Third St. (✆ **800/780-7234** or 573/248-1150; www.bestwestern.com).

WHY THEY'LL THANK YOU: Channeling an idyllic small-town childhood.

Presidential Homesteads

Presidential homesteads offer kids an opportunity to learn while they have fun and explore. Here are two homes where giants of history lived; but seeing their surroundings suddenly makes them human. It's a great way to illustrate to kids that history is made by real people, just like them.

72 Lincoln Trail   Driving the part of the Lincoln trail that covers Lincoln's early years will allow your kids to discover the backwoods boy behind the great president. The first stop is Hodgenville, Kentucky, at the **Abraham Lincoln Birthplace National Historical Park,** where a neoclassical memorial encloses a tiny log cabin, reportedly where Lincoln was born. Lincoln's humble origins are evident 7 miles north at the **Abraham Lincoln Boyhood Home,** a reconstruction of the cabin he lived in from ages 2 to 7. Drive 135 miles, and you'll find yourself in Lincoln City, Indiana—home of the **Lincoln Boyhood National Memorial,** a living history farm that recreates early 19th century farm life. *Abraham Lincoln Birthplace Historical Park:* ✆ *270/358-3137; www.nps.gov/abli. Lincoln Boyhood National Memorial:* ✆ *812/937-4541; www.nps.gov/libo.*

73 FDR Hyde Park   Franklin D. Roosevelt's lifelong home, Springwood, was a modest farmhouse when FDR's father built it. Franklin expanded it in an eclectic Dutch colonial style, giving it an imposing redbrick porticoed facade. He entertained Winston Churchill, King George VI, Queen Elizabeth of England, and many other dignitaries here. He also designed his own presidential library, the nation's first. A wooded trail leads from Springwood to their pair of private cottages where FDR and Eleanor could escape the pressures of political life. They are buried in the rose garden on the grounds. ✆ *800/FDR-VISIT [337-8474]; www.nps.gov/hofr.*

Yosemite
Rock-Climbing Heaven

Ages 8 & up • Yosemite, California

MOST FOLKS VISITING YOSEMITE NATIONAL PARK DON'T SEEM TO realize that there's more to it than Yosemite Valley, where crowds of cars and RVs inch along the roads while their passengers stare at the 3,000-foot-high glacier-carved granite walls and the waterfalls that drop down them. Yes, you should drive past the awesome 7,549-foot-high sheer rock face called **El Capitan;** you should pull off the road to take the easy half-mile trails to view **Bridalveil Fall** or **Lower Yosemite Falls.** But don't stop there—go up into the high country, where you can explore wilderness without the crowds.

The eastern half of 39-mile-long **Tioga Road** is open only in summer and fall, and the developed area around **Tuolumne Meadows** is much less crowded than Yosemite Valley. Coming from the west, Tioga Road rises up through towering pines and then breaks out on solid granite highlands dramatically furrowed by glaciers. Around Olmsted Point, the views become really dramatic—look at a cliff jutting up in the distance, and you'll realize that the ants scaling it are actually rock climbers. Yosemite is the most popular rock-climbing destination in the United States, thanks largely to the **Yosemite Mountaineering School** (✆ **209/372-8344;** www.yosemitemountaineering.com). The climbing school runs beginner classes daily out of its base in popular Curry Village, but in summer you can also take classes at Tuolumne Meadows. Kids as young as 10 are accepted in group classes (for your adventurous younger child, book a private lesson), and instructors will soon have your teenagers inching up the granite walls to heights of 60 feet.

Even children who are too young to scale a sheer rock face can get a little climbing experience in Yosemite's high country. From Tuolumne Meadows Lodge, a 4.2-mile trail leads to the top of **Lembert Dome** (take a shuttle bus back to the lodge from the trail's other end). Another option is off of Glacier Point Road, south of the Yosemite Valley loop. You'll want to drive this road anyway to get

Half Dome in Yosemite National Park.

to that great Glacier Point overlook, the top of a 3,200-foot vertical cliff. But stop partway along Glacier Point Road at mile 13.2, where a trail head leads 2.2 miles round-trip to **Sentinel Dome,** one of many granite domes in the park whose rounded shapes were formed by glaciers moving over them. It's 8,122 feet high, the second-highest viewpoint into the valley. **Taft Point** is the same distance the other way from the trail head; it has weird and scary cracks as well as cliff-overhang views. The hike itself isn't threatening, but hold hands near the end.

ⓘ Entrances on CA 41, CA 120, and CA 140 (℡ **209/372-0200;** www.nps.gov/yose).

✈ Fresno Yosemite International, 90 miles.

🛏 $$$ **The Ahwahnee,** Yosemite Valley (℡ **801/559-4884** or 209/372-1407; www.yosemitepark.com). $ **Tuolumne Meadows Campground** (℡ **800/436-7275;** www.recreation.gov).

WHY THEY'LL THANK YOU: Being on those peaks, not just looking at them.

Walking the Appalachian Trail

Ages 8 & up • White Mountains, New Hampshire

FOR THE ULTIMATE FAMILY BONDING ADVENTURE, NOTHING QUITE equals a hike along the Appalachian Trail. No, I'm not suggesting you do the whole rugged 2,100 miles of the Trail, which runs from Maine to Georgia. But you can conquer a segment of it, and one I'd recommend runs 56 miles through the White Mountain National Forest, where the nonprofit **Appalachian Mountain Club (AMC)** runs a unique network of eight huts, each a day's walk apart. Providing food and bedding, they let you travel light, reduced to backpacking essentials: some warm clothes, foul-weather gear, water, snacks. You'll be amid some of the most spectacular scenery in the

Looking down the Swift River in the White Mountains.

East—no trash, trailers, or loud music (the curse of overcrowded national park campgrounds), just room for kids to explore the world with new friends, kicking dust, balancing on fallen trees, and learning that when it rains you can't always change the channel.

My personal favorite family hike is a 3-day excursion up **Mount Lafayette.** Begin on the Franconia Notch Parkway (I-93), about 7½ miles north of Lincoln, New Hampshire, where you'll find the sign-post for the Old Bridle Path trail head. It's a sometimes-steep 2.9-mile hike from the road to the **Greenleaf Hut,** just above timberline at 4,200 feet, a warm, friendly place on Lafayette's west slope. When we last visited, the cook banged a pot with a heavy metal spoon at 6pm sharp, and we joined about 25 others—a lively mingling of singles, couples, and families—at long wooden tables for a very honest chicken-and-vegetable stew, with homemade bread and a mysterious pudding. After dinner, we sat on a rocky ledge and watched the evening mist flow through the valley below.

Next morning is your main hiking day: Climb 1.1 miles to the rocky, often windswept summit of Mount Lafayette. The payoff, on clear days, is the 1.7-mile (1-hr.) walk from Lafayette along a narrow ridge, with the whole Franconia range stretched below you, to Little Haystack. Retrace your steps to the Greenleaf Hut for your second night. On the morning of the third day, return to your car, an easy 2-hour downhill hike.

Other AMC huts that are popular with families are the **Zealand Falls Hut,** a 2.8-mile walk to a choice four-season spot near waterfalls, perfect for moose spotting; and the even more accessible **Lonesome Lake Hut,** a painless 1.7-mile hike to a lake. Guided hut-to-hut trips can also be arranged.

(i) © 603/745-3816; www.fs.fed.us/r9/forests/white_mountain.

✈ Boston Logan International, 130 miles to Lincoln, NH.

⊨ Contact **Appalachian Mountain Club** (© **603/466-2727;** www.outdoors.org).

WHY THEY'LL THANK YOU: The joy of reaching the summit—together.

Getting Past the Crowds in Yellowstone

All ages • Entrances at Gardiner & West Yellowstone,
Montana, and Jackson & Cody, Wyoming

Every visitor to Yellowstone National Park wants to see the park's signature attraction, the **Old Faithful** geyser, which erupts about every 90 minutes. You can drive to Old Faithful on the Lower Loop Road from the park's west entrance and join the crowds of tourists sitting on benches waiting for this baby to blow. Another popular drive-up sight is the limestone terraces of **Mammoth Hot Springs,** near the north entrance, where masses of bacteria and algae in the thermal water turn the rocks orange, pink, yellow, green, and brown. But these two sights only scratch the surface of Yellowstone's geothermal features, if you're willing to get out and do some hiking to see them.

You'll have the geysers practically to yourself if you head for the **Shoshone Geyser Basin,** which begins a mile west of Shoshone Lake (find a trail head for **DeLacey Creek Trail** on the road 8 miles east of Old Faithful; it leads 3 miles to Shoshone Lake). The **North Shoshone Trail** passes 26 campsites as it winds through a lodgepole-pine forest. The **Bechler River Trail** in the park's southwest corner is rich in waterfalls, cascades, and thermal areas. If its wildlife you're after, try the **Sportsman Lake Trail,** which passes through sagebrush plateaus full of elk and a meadow popular with moose.

Yellowstone is also one of the country's best places for families to go backpacking. Some beautiful campsites are just a couple miles off the road, and it only takes a walk of 20 minutes or so before you feel gloriously alone with the bison, elk, and other wildlife. Some great family trails for day hikes include these: at Mammoth, the 5-mile **Beaver Ponds Loop** from the hot springs at Liberty Cap (go in the evening or early morning to see the beavers); the 6-mile round-trip hike up **Mount Washburn,** an alpine trail leading to a 10,243-foot-high view over much of Yellowstone

The Grand Canyon of the Yellowstone.

(watch for bighorn sheep); and the **Clear Lake Trail** from the Wapiti trail head, which wanders through beautiful rolling meadows to a strange body of water fed by hot springs.

The backcountry season here is short—mid-June through the end of August, when the snow has finally melted off and streams drop to fordable levels—so it's wise to make a campsite reservation way in advance.

ⓘ ✆ **307/344-7381;** www.nps.gov/yell. **Yellowstone Backcountry Office** (✆ **307/344-2160**).

✈ Yellowstone, West Yellowstone, MT, 2 miles. Yellowstone Regional, Cody, WY, 52 miles.

⊨ $ **Madison Hotel,** 139 Yellowstone Ave., West Yellowstone, MT (✆ **800/838-7745** or 406/646-7745; www.madisonhotelmotel. com). $$ **Mammoth Hot Springs Hotel** (✆ **866/439-7375** or 307/ 344-7311; www.travelyellowstone.com).

BEST TIME: June to September.

WHY THEY'LL THANK YOU: Learning to tell an elk from a moose.

Cycling   **77**

Bicycling on Nantucket
All ages • Nantucket, Massachusetts

BRINGING A CAR TO NANTUCKET, THE TINY MASSACHUSETTS ISLAND 30 miles off Cape Cod, can be an incredible hassle in summer—there are only six pokey car ferries per day from Hyannis, and they book up months in advance. Day visitors generally choose to come on foot (which frees you to opt for a high-speed ferry), but then they don't explore any farther than tourist-mobbed Nantucket Town. Your solution? Rent bikes. Flat, sandy Nantucket is heaven for beginning bicyclists, with paved paths leading all over. Bring helmets with you (they're required for children under 12) or rent them along with bikes in Nantucket Town at shops right by the wharf (visit www.wheelsheelsandpedals.com for more information). Nothing could be easier, or more fun.

Here's the lay of the land: Three major bike routes radiate out from Nantucket Town, one heading west to **Madaket,** 6¼ miles, one south to **Surfside** 3½ miles, and the longest one a 17-mile loop out to **Siasconset Beach** ('Sconset to locals) and **Sankaty Head lighthouse.** It's classic beachy terrain, with few trees, wide skies, and swaths of tall dune grass on both sides. The pedaling is easy, and the island's small scale makes you feel you're really getting somewhere, especially when you hit the bluffs and get that Atlantic panorama. Picnic benches and water fountains are conveniently provided at strategic points along all the paths, which you'll appreciate if you're towing really young ones in a bike trailer.

Madaket is picturesque, especially at sunset, but has strong surf; with kids, you're better off turning right on Eel Point Road and swimming at gentler Dionis Beach. Popular **Surfside beach** is your best bet with young children, not only because the ride is shorter but because there's a snack bar. My favorite, though, is the ride to **'Sconset,** even though it is the most demanding, longer and with a few hills. 'Sconset is rarely, if ever, crowded, perhaps because of the water's strong sideways tow. Lifeguards are usually on duty, but the closest facilities (restrooms, grocery store, and cafe) are back in the center of the village, which is lovely and worth a stop anyway. From 'Sconset, head north along the coastal path on Polpis Road, stopping off to snap Nantucket photos in front of the classic lighthouse at Sankaty Head. If you've planned ahead, though, you've booked an unforgettable naturalist-led tour (offered June–Oct) of the barrier beaches with the **Coskata-Coatue Wildlife Refuge** (✆ **508/228-6799;** www.thetrustees.org; reservation required); detour up Wauwinet Road to the Wauwinet Gate House to meet the tour. By the time you pedal back into Nantucket Town and get back on the ferry, you'll have spent a day in the sun you won't soon forget.

ⓘ **Nantucket Visitor Services,** 25 Federal St. (✆ **508/228-0925;** www.nantucket-ma.gov).

🛏 $$ **Jared Coffin House,** 29 Broad St. (✆ **800/248-2405** or 508/228-2400; www.jaredcoffinhouse.com).

WHY THEY'LL THANK YOU: A first taste of bike touring that'll leave them wanting more.

Cycling 78

Mackinac Island
Not a Car in Sight
All ages • Straits of Mackinac, Michigan

CROPPING OUT OF THE STRAITS OF MACKINAC, WHICH SEPARATE THE Upper and Lower peninsulas of Michigan at their closest point, this summer resort island is a Victorian period piece of white frame houses and trim gardens. The only way to reach it is by private plane or ferry; and since you can't bring a car, you have three options for getting around the island: on foot, by horse-drawn carriage, and on a bike. Pedaling happily along the limestone cliffs overlooking the straits, you may wonder why the automobile was ever invented.

A complete circuit of the island on traffic-free **Lake Shore Road** only takes 8 miles, doable even with fairly young riders (rental bikes in town also offer child seats and trailers if that's a better option for you). You'll have to stop along the way, of course, to drink in the views—don't miss Arch Rock on the east coast, a boulder pierced with a gaping 30- by 40-foot hole gouged by waves and glaciers, or Sunset Rock on the west bluff above town. Most of the island is covered by **Mackinac Island State Park** (© 906/847-6330; www.mackinacparks.com), with 70 miles of paved roads and trails where cyclists can explore the cedar- and birch-forested interior. Above the town, you can also cycle up to **Fort Mackinac** (7127 Huron Rd.), built by British soldiers during the American Revolution to defend the link between Lakes Michigan and Huron, vital to the lucrative fur trade. Fourteen buildings, mostly from the 1880s, are still intact, and costumed interpreters do military reenactments; shoot off rifles and cannons; lead children's games; and perform bugle, fife-and-drum, and bagpipe music. The cliff-top site was chosen specifically for sentries to watch over the lakes, so you can just imagine how fantastic the views are.

Of course, if you'd rather take in the scenery from a rocking chair, you can always plunk yourself down on the white colonnaded

Mackinac Island.

veranda—the world's longest front porch—of the landmark **Grand Hotel** (see below), built in 1887. Even if you're not staying here, you can tour the historic hotel. In the center of town, a few neat low white buildings recall the days of the early-18th-century fur traders, along with a bark chapel built by the original Huron natives.

ⓘ **Mackinac Island Chamber of Commerce** (ℂ 800/454-5227 or 906/847-3783; www.mackinacisland.org).

✈ Pellston Regional, 15 miles from Mackinaw City ferry docks.

🛏 $$$ **Grand Hotel,** West Bluff Rd. (ℂ **800/33-GRAND** [334-7263] or 906/847-3331; www.grandhotel.com). $$ **Mission Point Resort,** 6633 Main St. (ℂ **800/833-7711** or 906/847-3312; www.missionpoint.com).

BEST TIME: May to October.

WHY THEY'LL THANK YOU: Overtaking a carriage, your bikes will be the fastest things on the road.

Crater Lake
Cycling the Rim Road
Ages 8 & up • Crater Lake, Oregon

THE STORY BEGINS WITH A VOLCANIC EXPLOSION SO FEARSOME— scientists estimate it was 42 times as powerful as Mount St. Helens— that it left behind a phenomenally deep crater, which in time filled with water to become America's deepest lake. But this version of events doesn't prepare you for the sight of Crater Lake, for the intense sapphire blue of its cold spring-fed waters reflecting the sheer forested cliffs that encircle it. It's simply breathtaking, a panorama of supreme serenity that belies its violent origins. It takes about 2 hours to drive around Crater Lake—which, unfortunately, is all most park visitors do, rolling along the asphalt, narcotized by the pretty scenery. Trade in those four wheels for two, though, and you'll really feel the transforming power of this volcanic landscape.

The 33-mile **Rim Drive,** open only in summer, has 30 overlooks where you can gaze at these pristine waters cupped in their rocky chalice. Travel clockwise, wear bright clothing so motorists can spot you, and if possible sleep in the park the night before so you can hit the narrow road early before the traffic gets heavy (as it inevitably will). The Rim Drive may look like an easy pedal, but don't underestimate it—it can be demanding, especially on the east side of the lake, where there are more hills (hills you'd scarcely notice if you were just driving). On the other hand, the east side of the lake has more panoramic views, providing good excuses to catch your breath. The **Cloudcap Overlook** is 2,000 feet high, with vistas that stretch as far as Mount Shasta. Another cool turnoff overlooks the **Phantom Ship,** a jagged basalt formation jutting up out of the lake.

An alternative ride goes from the **Rim Village Visitor Center** north to the **Cleetwood Cove Trailhead** and back, 21 miles total, on the flatter west rim. Cleetwood Cove is the sole trail that goes down to the lake's edge; it may only be 2.2 miles round-trip, but the way back is strenuous, like climbing 65 flights of stairs. My advice: Save your strength for the cycling.

No matter which of the park's entrances you come in, you'll drive a few miles to get to the Rim Drive, where you can park your car and get the bikes off your rack. If you've got more than one driver in your party, consider taking turns driving the car to meet the cyclists at each overlook—it'll give the kids the option of pooping out if necessary. (Blame it on the high altitude.) There are no bike rentals in the park, but you can rent them at **Diamond Lake Resort,** 5 miles from the park's north entrance on OR 138 (✆ **800/733-7593** or 541/793-3333; www.diamondlake.net).

ⓘ Along OR 62 (✆ **541/594-3000;** www.nps.gov/crla).

✈ Rogue Valley International-Medford, 80 miles.

🛏 $$$ **Crater Lake Lodge,** Rim Rd. (✆ **888/774-CRATER** [774-2728] or 541/830-8700; www.craterlakelodges.com). $ **Mazama Village Campground,** in the park, off OR 62 (✆ **888/774-CRATER** [774-2728] or 541/830-8700; www.craterlakelodges.com).

BEST TIME: Late June to September.

WHY THEY'LL THANK YOU: Discovering how rugged this pretty place really is.

80 In the Saddle

Rocky Mountain National Park
Trail Riding on the Roof of the World
Ages 6 & up • Near Estes Park, Colorado

CHANCES ARE YOU'VE NEVER BEEN AS CLOSE TO THE SKY AS YOU'LL BE at **Rocky Mountain National Park,** most of which is at least 8,000 feet high. Up here, the air is so thin and cool you'll feel giddy, the sun's UV rays so intense that sun block and sunglasses are a must.

It's a land of ponderosa pine, gnarled alpine tundra, heathery slopes, bare granite, dizzying views, and so many elk they'll browse right up to your campground. The Continental Divide slices across the middle of this compact park—you can drive over it on Trail Ridge Road, that stretch of U.S. 34 that cuts across the park east to west—it's 48 miles of truly spectacular mountaintop views, much of it above the timberline. The park also has laid out several short nature trails that kids will enjoy—check park maps for the **Moraine Park Nature Trail,** the **Sprague Lake Nature Trail,** and the **Bear Lake Trail;** the **Beaver Boardwalk** near the beginning of **Trail Ridge Road** is a great place to scout out dam-building beavers.

But the best way to plunge into this wilderness is to swing into a Western saddle and take a ride on horseback. Ever since this park was founded in 1915, it's been a popular high-country riding area. While many national parks offer only a standard 1-hour circle ride, at Rocky Mountain you can take guided trail rides from 2 to 8 hours, or even book overnight pack trips; early-morning trail rides that include a cowboy breakfast are always a hit with kids. An ample

Rocky Mountain National Park.

network of worn dirt trails—some 260 miles of them—wind into the glacier-carved countryside past steep, craggy mountain slopes and small, round reflecting lakes. Children as young as 6 can have a horse to themselves, while younger children ride with a parent.

There are stables all over the area, several of them run by **Sombrero Ranch Stables** (✆ **970/586-4577;** www.sombrero.com). On the more developed eastern side of the park, there's one at Moraine Park (✆ **970/586-2327**), another near the Glacier Basin Campground on Sprague Lake (✆ **970/586-3244**), and one just outside the park opposite Lake Estes Dam on U.S. 34 (✆ **970/586-4577**). On the west side of the park, there's another just outside park boundaries in the Grand Lake area (✆ **970/627-3514**). Also in Grand Lake, the family-oriented Winding River Resort (see below) offers 1- and 2-hour trail rides, plus pony rides for younger riders.

ⓘ U.S. 34 or U.S. 36 (✆ **970/586-1206;** www.nps.gov/romo).

✈ Denver International, 65 miles.

🛏 $$$ **Glacier Lodge,** 2166 Tunnel Rd. (CO 66), Estes Park, south of park entrance (✆ **800/523-3920** or 970/586-4401; www.glacier lodge.com). $$ **Winding River Resort,** 1441 C.R. 491, Grand Lake (✆ **800/282-5121,** 970/627-3215, or 303/623-1121; www.winding riverresort.com).

BEST TIME: Mid-May to mid-September.

WHY THEY'LL THANK YOU: The clip-clop of hooves echoing off the top of the world.

Monument Valley
The Iconic Wild West Landscape

Ages 6 & up • Kayenta, Arizona

WHEN MOST OF US THINK OF THE AMERICAN WEST, THIS IS WHAT clicks into our mental View-Masters: a vast, flat sagebrush plain with huge sandstone spires thrusting to the sky like the fingers of ancient Mother Earth clutching for the heavens. Ever since movie director John Ford first started shooting westerns here in the 1930s, this landscape has felt familiar to millions who have never set foot here. (Just outside the park, **Goulding's Trading Post Museum** recreates the era in the 1920s and 1930s when the moviemakers first discovered the area.) We've all seen it on the big screen, but oh, what a difference to see it in real life.

Because the park is on Navajo tribal lands—their name for it is Tsebii'nidzisgai, "the valley within the rocks"—there are only three ways to tour the area: driving the 17-mile Valley Drive past 11 photo-op overlooks; taking an off-road jeep tour with a Navajo guide; or on guided hikes and trail rides, which range from 1-hour loops to 8-hour excursions. The classic way to experience these dramatic scrublands, of course, is from on a Western saddle, the way John Wayne saw it. The native guides, born and bred to this barren landscape, will not only lead the ride, they'll help you appreciate the intricate beauties of this landscape, which is sacred to their tribe. One of the most comprehensive tour companies (jeeps, hikes, horses, you name it) is **Sacred Monument Tours** (✆ **435/727-3218;** www.monumentvalley.net). Many of the trail rides follow the Mittens trail, which heads north to Sentinel Mesa and then comes back along the floor of the West Mitten mesa; longer rides add on the Castle Butte, Stage Coach, or Big Indian Spire mesas. Another popular option for more experienced riders goes into backcountry, outside the official park boundaries, to visit Teardrop Arch and Horseshoe Canyon. If you possibly can, time your visit to

Monument Valley.

include sunset—as the sheer walls of these monoliths capture the light of the setting sun, they truly seem to catch fire.

As you stare at them, take an extra moment to imagine the forces of nature that have sculpted the soft desert stone into these incredible shapes. It's an only-in-America panorama that the kids won't ever forget.

ⓘ Monument Valley Navajo Tribal Park, U.S. 163, 30 miles north of Kayenta (🕻 **435/727-5874**; www.navajonationparks.org/htm/monumentvalley.htm).

✈ Flagstaff Pulliam, 180 miles.

🛏 $$ **Goulding's Lodge,** Monument Valley, UT (🕻 **435/727-3231**; www.gouldings.com). $$ **Hampton Inn Kayenta,** U.S. 160, Kayenta, AZ (🕻 **800/HAMPTON** [426-7866] or 928/697-3170; www.hampton-inn.com or www.monumentvalleyonline.com).

WHY THEY'LL THANK YOU: Just like the movies—only more so.

Canoeing the Everglades
Paddling through a River of Grass
Ages 6 & up • Florida City or Everglades City, Florida

THE EVERGLADES IS A BIZARRE ECOSYSTEM, WHEN YOU THINK ABOUT it: a drawling grassy river that's rarely more than knee-deep, but spreads some 40 miles wide, harboring an exotic population of manatees, hawksbill turtles, water moccasins, coral snakes, panthers, armadillos, muskrats, opossums, river otters, herons, egrets, the roseate spoonbill, and the big black anhinga bird. It's the only place in the world where alligators and crocodiles live side by side. There's nothing like it anywhere else—and it might not be here much longer, given the encroaching development in southern Florida. Bring the kids here now, to dip a paddle into this River of Grass while it still flows.

While you can stick to dry land—driving or biking on the paved park roads, or walking short nature trails through junglelike patches of forest—the whole point of this place is that it *isn't* dry land. What you really want is to feel the sway and lap of the park's waters, the lazy grace of its fluid meander through mangroves and cypresses and sawgrass prairies. Rent canoes at the **Gulf Coast Visitor Center,** on FL 29 in Everglades City (✆ **239/695-3311**), or the **Flamingo Lodge** by the Flamingo Visitor Center, at the end of S.R. 9336 at the southern tip of the park (✆ **239/695-2945**). In a canoe you'll be incredibly close to the water level, casually coexisting with gators and birds as if you're part of their natural environment. That just won't happen on those powered airboats that offer Everglades tours just outside park boundaries. (They aren't allowed in the park proper.)

Everglades National Park's longest "trails" are designed for canoe travel, and many are marked as clearly as walking trails. From the Gulf Coast, you can canoe 2 miles across **Chokoloskee Bay** to a mangrove island, or follow the **Turner River** 8 miles from freshwater cypress forest into saltwater mangrove swamp. From

Flamingo, the **Noble Hammock Canoe Trail** is an easy 2-mile loop; the **Hell's Bay Canoe Trail** is 3 to 6 miles, depending on how far you venture. A guided boat tour is a great idea, not only to find your way but to benefit from the guide's familiarity with the flora and fauna; contact **Everglades National Park Boat Tours,** at the Park's Docks on Chokoloskee Causeway (S.R. 29) in Everglades City (📞 **239/695-2591**), or **North American Canoe Tours** at the Ivey House B&B (see below; www.evergladesadventures.com).

ⓘ **Ernest F. Coe Visitor Center,** 40001 S.R. 9336, west of Florida City in Homestead (📞 **305/242-7700;** www.nps.gov/ever).

✈ Miami International, 40 miles.

🛏 $$ **Best Western Gateway to the Keys,** 411 S. Krome Ave., Florida City (📞 **888/981-5100** or 305/246-5100; www.bestwestern. com). $$ **Ivey House B&B,** 107 Camellia St., Everglades City (📞 **877/ 567-0679** or 239/695-3299; www.iveyhouse.com).

BEST TIME: Dry season (winter or spring).

WHY THEY'LL THANK YOU: Gliding through the glassy, grassy silence.

Paddling Away

83

Sea Kayaking in Acadia National Park
The Maine Way to Enjoy the Coast
Ages 8 & up • Mount Desert Island, Maine

MAINE'S MOUNT DESERT ISLAND IS HOME TO SPECTACULAR ACADIA National Park, a rich glacier-carved mound of rugged cliffs, restless ocean, and quiet woods. Mount Desert (pronounced des-*sert*) is surrounded by small bays and coast-hugging islands and nearly knifed in half by narrow, 7-mile-long Somes Sound, the only true fjord in the continental United States. Most visitors crowd onto 20-mile **Park Loop Road,** a spectacular drive that starts near the **Hulls Cove Visitor Center** and follows the rocky coast past pictur- esque coves, looping back inland along **Jordan Pond** and **Eagle Lake** with a detour to **Cadillac Mountain**—a sort of greatest-hits tour of the island. But why spend your time poking along in traffic, staring out at the ocean, when you could be skimming along the water's surface, skirting the coast and exploring the coves in your own light and agile sea kayak?

Frenchman's Bay, where the island's main town, **Bar Harbor,** sits, is a great place for youngsters to learn how to kayak, sitting in the front seat of a flat, stable two-person kayak with a parent pad- dling in back. Head south from the bay and you'll reach Atlantic waters, where popular park sights include **Thunder Hole,** a shal- low cavern where the surf surges boisterously in and out, and **Otter Cliffs,** a set of 100-foot-high granite precipices capped with dense spruce that plummet down into roiling seas. From your kayak you can also enjoy open views of waterside villages and the great shingled "cottages" of the wealthy elite—Carnegies, Rocke- fellers, Astors, Vanderbilts—who summered here in the island's late-19th-century heyday as a resort.

Outfitters offer a variety of options, from a 2½-hour harbor tour to a 7-hour excursion. **Coastal Kayaking Tours,** 48 Cottage St., Bar Harbor (© **800/526-8615** or 207/288-9605; www.acadiafun. com), has a 4-hour outing tailored for families with children as young as 8. Experienced kayakers can set out on their own with rentals from **Acadia 1 Watersports,** 1564 Shore Rd., Lamoine (© **888/786-0676** or 207/677-2963; www.kayak1.com), or **Aqua- terra Adventures,** 1 West St., Bar Harbor (© **877/386-4124** or 207/288-0007; www.aquaterra-adventures.com).

Frenchman's Bay is populated by seals, osprey, and other wildlife; in early fall, huge flocks of eider ducks can sometimes be seen float- ing just off the Atlantic shore. Summer boasts even more spectacu- lar wildlife: humpback, finback, minke, and (occasionally) right whales, which migrate to cool summer waters offshore to feast on krill and plankton. For a closer look you can take an excursion with the **Bar Harbor Whale Watch Company,** 1 West St., Bar Harbor (© **800/942-5374** or 207/288-2386; www.barharborwhales.com).

ⓘ **Hulls Cove Visitor Center,** Rte. 3 (✆ **207/288-3338;** www. nps.gov/acad).

✈ Hancock County–Bar Harbor, Trenton, just across the causeway from Mount Desert Island. Bangor International, 41 miles.

🛏 $ **Bar Harbor Campground,** 409 State Hwy. 3, Salisbury Cove (✆ **207/288-5185;** www.thebarharborcampground.com). $$$ **Harborside Hotel & Marina,** 55 West St., Bar Harbor (✆ **800/ 328-5033** or 207/288-5033; www.theharborsidehotel.com).

WHY THEY'LL THANK YOU: Skimming over steel-blue seas, swift as an osprey.

Paddling Away

84

Apostle Islands National Lakeshore
Seeing the Great Lakes by Kayak
Ages 8 & up • Bayfield, Wisconsin

THE OLD FRENCH EXPLORERS, THE ORIGINAL VOYAGEURS WHO PADDLED across North America in the 1600s seeking fur-trapping riches, probably would have used sea kayaks instead of canoes if they'd only known. A closed cockpit boat like a kayak is exactly what you want in order to venture onto the cold, often rough waters of Lake Superior, the largest freshwater lake in the world. Come here in the summertime and the waters aren't quite so cold, though the waves are still unpredictable. But you're snug in your kayak and you can ride it out just fine.

Right off the northernmost tip of Wisconsin lies a scatter of 22 forested islands—on the map it almost looks as if the Bayfield Peninsula had sneezed them out into Lake Superior—and boaters have long found island-hopping in these frigid (but relatively shallow) waters an irresistible temptation. The Apostle Islands National Lakeshore headquarters lies on the tip of the Bayfield peninsula, but that's merely an anchor point—most of the park is accessible only by boat. Let the kids look at a map and choose day-trip destinations within easy kayaking distance—historic island lighthouses, shipwreck sites, abandoned brownstone quarries, a ruined one-room schoolhouse, inviting sand beaches. Red sandstone cliffs line the otherwise woodsy shore, with sea caves in their bases that only kayaks can explore.

Local outfitters offer rentals, kayaking instruction (usually in protected bays or inland lakes rather than Superior itself), and guided excursions, both day trips and overnights—unless you're already experienced kayakers, having a guide is a huge plus, allowing you to paddle directly to the most interesting sights. (The sea caves in particular can be treacherous to visit if you don't know the waters well.) Outfitters include **Living Adventure** (© 866/779-9503 or 715/779-9503; www.livingadventure.com), **Trek & Trail** (© 800/354-8735; www.trek-trail.com), and **Whitecap Kayak** (© 906/364-7336; www.whitecapkayak.com).

If your kayaking skills aren't enough to get you out onto the islands, never fear—you can always go there on narrated trips run by **Apostle Islands Cruises** (© 800/323-7619 or 715/779-3925; www.apostleisland.com), departing from the Bayfield city dock.

ⓘ **Bayfield Visitor Center,** 415 Washington Ave., Bayfield (© **715/779-3397;** www.nps.gov/apis).

✈ Sawyer County, Hayward, WI, 75 miles. Gogebic–Iron County, Bessemer, MI, 75 miles.

🛏 $$ **Bayfield Inn,** 20 Rittenhouse Ave. (© **800/382-0995** or 715/779-3363; www.bayfieldinn.com). $$ **Winfield Inn,** 225 E. Lynde Ave. (© **715/779-3252;** www.winfieldinn.com).

BEST TIME: May to September.

WHY THEY'LL THANK YOU: Feeling like a voyager.

Vieques
Swimming with a Million Tiny Lights
Ages 4 & up • Puerto Rico

I THOUGHT PUERTO RICO WAS AN ISLAND—BUT HOW CAN AN ISLAND have an island? Well, Puerto Rico has two, Vieques and Culebra, for years a well-kept secret among Puerto Ricans themselves, who come here to escape the tourists on the big island. Since the U.S. Navy, in 2003, closed its installation on Vieques, though, much more land is available for vacationers, and Vieques is rapidly becoming known as an ecofriendly—and still charmingly scruffy—destination.

With some 40 palm-lined white-sand beaches, and reefs of snorkel-worthy antler coral off shore, Vieques—11km (6¾ miles) off the big island's east coast, only an hour by ferry—has an obvious appeal for sun-loving families. But one of the coolest things on Vieques has nothing at all to do with the sun. Just west of the main town, Isabel Segunda, lies **Mosquito Bay,** which has been renamed Phosphorescent Bay for the way its waters glow in the dark, thanks to millions of tiny bioluminescent organisms called pyrodiniums (translation from science-speak: "whirling fire"). They're only about one-five-hundredth of an inch in size, but when these tiny swimming creatures are disturbed (by, for example, a hovering tour boat), they dart away and light up like fireflies, leaving eerie blue-white trails of phosphorescence. These pyrodiniums exist elsewhere, but not in such amazing concentrations: A gallon of water in Mosquito Bay may contain upward of three-quarters of a million such creatures. It's definitely worth letting the kids stay up late for once. Wear a bathing suit because it's possible to swim in these glowing waters. Don't make the mistake of coming here on a full moon, however—the glow of the pyrodiniums is only discernible on a cloudy, moonless night. (**Warning:** Some tour boats go out to the bay regardless of the full moon—and you won't get your money back if you're disappointed.)

159

Island Adventures (☎ 787/741-0720; www.biobay.com) operates 2-hour nighttime trips in Phosphorescent Bay aboard the Luminosa, though not during the full moon. If the kids are into kayaking, they can get even closer to those glow-in-the-dark waters on a kayak tour offered by **Blue Caribe Kayaks** (☎ 787/741-2522; www.bluecaribekayaks. com). In fact, Blue Caribe acts as a clearinghouse for all the island's watersports outfitters—it's a small island, and virtually everybody is related to everyone else. That small-town casualness is one of the things that still makes Vieques a great place for traveling families, hot spot or not.

Palm-lined beach on Vieques.

ⓘ www.enchanted-isle.com.

FERRY: Puerto Rico Port Authority, Fajardo, P.R., to Isabel Segunda, Vieques (1¼ hr.; ☎ **800/981-2005,** 787/863-0705 in Fajardo, or 787/741-4761 in Vieques).

🛌 $$ **The Crow's Nest,** Rte. 201, Barrio Florida (☎ **877/CROWS-NEST** [276-9763] or 787/741-0033; www.crowsnestvieques.com). $$ **Trade Winds Guest House,** Calle Flamboyan 107, Esperanza (☎ **787/741-8666;** www.tradewindsvieques.com).

WHY THEY'LL THANK YOU: Nature's night light.

86

Biscayne National Park
Florida's Homegrown Coral Reef
Ages 8 & up • Homestead, Florida

BISCAYNE NATIONAL PARK IS ONE OF THE LEAST-CROWDED PARKS in America's national park system, probably because its main attractions are kind of difficult to reach. It's not a question of being remote—it's so close to Miami, you can do it as a day trip—but more about being hidden from view. Above ground, you'll see only a no-big-deal strip of mangrove shoreline and 44 barrier islands, most of them mere specks off of South Florida's east coast. But beneath the surface lies the world's third-longest coral reef, an aquatic universe pulsing with multicolored life. All it takes is strapping on a snorkel and fins for kids to be able to cruise around this tropical paradise, encountering bright parrotfish and angelfish, gently rocking sea fans, and coral labyrinths.

The clear, warm waters of Biscayne National Park are packed with reef fish, rays, moray eels, jellyfish, anemones, sponges, even sea turtles and dolphins—some 512 species, all told, in this 173,000-acre expanse. On top of that, an **underwater trail** identifies six shipwrecks off of Elliott Key; mooring buoys point the way to the wrecks, with waterproof cards attached to tell the kids what they're seeing. You can rent equipment at the full-service dive shop at the park's mainland entrance at Convoy Point, and if you don't have your own boat, you can take a 3-hour snorkeling or diving tour operated every afternoon by **Biscayne National Underwater Park, Inc.,** 9700 SW 328th St. (✆ **305/230-1100;** www.biscayne underwater.com); you'll either stick to the bay or head out to the reefs, depending on the very changeable weather. Even beginning snorkelers will get a satisfying eyeful.

The mainland entrance is 9 miles east of Homestead, off U.S. 1; a small beach and marina are nearby, but the rest of the park is accessible only by boat, either your own or the park concession's water transport (✆ **305/230-1100**). Few of the park's islands are even open to visitors; the two most popular are Elliott Key and Boca Chita Key, which can be reached by launch from the visitor center. Both islands have campsites (call the park ranger at ☏ **305/ 230-7275** for information on permits and camping fees) and places to moor your boat; **Elliott Key** also has an interesting nature trail, and **Boca Chita,** once an exclusive haven for yachters, has some restored historic buildings.

If you prefer not to dive, take the wimp's way out and view the underwater sights on a 3-hour **glass-bottom boat tour** offered by Biscayne National Underwater Park, Inc., departing at 10am and at 1:30pm. Reservations are almost always necessary.

ⓘ **Dante Fascell Visitor Center,** at Convoy Point, 9700 SW 328th St. (☏ **305/230-7275;** www.nps.gov/bisc).

✈ Miami International, 40 miles.

🛏 $$ **Indian Creek Hotel,** 2727 Indian Creek Dr., Miami Beach (☏ **800/491-2772** or 305/531-2727; www.indiancreekhotel.com). $$$ **Ritz-Carlton Key Biscayne,** 455 Grand Bay Dr., Key Biscayne (☏ **800/542-8680** or 305/365-4500; www.ritzcarlton.com).

WHY THEY'LL THANK YOU: Tropical colors and eerie shipwrecks.

Snorkeling & Diving　**87**

St. John
Snorkeling on the Trunk Bay Trail
Ages 6 & up • U.S. Virgin Islands

THE FIRST PLACE MY KIDS EVER PUT A MASK AND SNORKEL INTO THE water was down here in the U.S. Virgin Islands, and I'm afraid it spoiled them for more ordinary snorkeling experiences. I still have photos of them standing on the white-sand beach at Cinnamon Bay, along with the five kids of the other families we were traveling with, looking like an invasion party of aliens in their rented snorkeling gear—eight breathing tubes sticking up like antennae, eight pairs of flippers shifting impatiently in the sand, and their masks making them look like eight frowning Cyclopes. We deliberately took forever getting that shot, just because it made them so antsy. Enough photos already, they wanted to get out in that turquoise water and *start snorkeling*.

Their snorkeling debuts took place where so many others have started out: at Trunk Bay, where the National Park Service has set up the **National Park Underwater Trail.** This 225-yard trail follows a reef where all the underwater features are labeled with signs 5 to 15 feet under the water's surface. Snorkeling snobs wouldn't be caught dead at popular Trunk Bay doing the trail—they prefer more remote places like Watermelon Cay or Salt Pond Bay or Haulover Bay, where the snorkeling's a lot more challenging—but with children, Trunk Bay is just the thing. The signs help to focus young snorkelers' attention and keep them going, and it was extremely helpful for them to learn the difference between various coral structures, between a sea fan and an anemone. As for the bright parrotfish flitting by, well, no sign can be attached to something that elusive, but since the signs had made the kids more attentive snorkelers, they spotted the parrotfish all right. They were hoping for sea turtles—hawksbills and leatherbacks are common in these waters—but the turtles sensibly kept their distance. With kids, we were also grateful for Trunk Bay's other amenities—flush toilets, a snack bar, and lifeguards.

We also just plain fell in love with St. John—with two-thirds of it protected as Virgin Islands National Park, it's remarkably unspoiled, with lots of dense foliage and hiking trails and unruffled quiet, surrounded by expanses of clear, sparkling turquoise waters. It's what we'd always expected the Caribbean to be—and now that we had the kids hooked on snorkeling, our island-hopping days could begin.

ⓘ **Virgin Islands National Park,** Trunk Bay (✆ **340/776-6201;** www.nps.gov/viis).

✈ Cyril E. King, St. Thomas, 45–60 min. by boat.

🛏 $$ **Cinnamon Bay Campground,** Cruz Bay (✆ **800/539-9998** or 340/776-6330; www.cinnamonbay.com). $$$ **Westin St. John Resort,** Great Cruz Bay (✆ **866/716-8108** or 340/693-8000; www.westinresortstjohn.com).

WHY THEY'LL THANK YOU: Connecting the dots underwater.

Santa Monica Beach
The Golden Essence of Beachy California

All ages • Santa Monica, California

PLANNING OUR MOST RECENT TRIP TO SOUTHERN CALIFORNIA, MY KIDS envisioned a classic white-sand beach with the Pacific Ocean sparkling blue-green beyond and a gentle white-fringed surf they could jump in to their heart's content. It was ridiculously easy for us to fulfill that fantasy with a lazy afternoon at Santa Monica State Beach (off the Pacific Coast Hwy.). What's not to like? Even on a summer Sunday, this wide strand was blissfully uncrowded; restrooms, yes, tacky food stands, no. We could even bicycle up here on the paved beach path from funky Venice Beach, where the vibe is edgier but the sand and surf not nearly so nice. Santa Monica Beach has big parking lots and nearby cafes. It's one of those cases where hunting for the exotic is a waste of time: Santa Monica Beach is easy to get to, free, and sparkling clean, an ideal place for a quintessential California day at the beach.

Just south of the beach you can visit the **Santa Monica Pier,** Ocean Avenue at the end of Colorado Avenue (✆ **310/458-8900;** www.santamonicapier.org), one of the last of Southern California's vintage seaside piers. The Santa Monica Pier evokes the area's 19th-century seaside resort days, long before Los Angeles became La-La Land. Built in 1908 for passenger and cargo ships, the wooden wharf is now home to seafood restaurants and snack shacks, a touristy Mexican cantina, and a gaily colored turn-of-the-20th-century indoor wooden carousel (which Paul Newman operated in *The Sting*). A small amusement area perched halfway down, **Pacific Park** (✆ **310/260-8744;** www.pacpark.com), hearkens back to the granddaddy pier amusement park in California, Pacific Ocean Park; this updated version has a Ferris wheel, roller coaster, and other rides, right on the ocean's edge. Anglers head to the pier's end to fish, and nostalgia buffs to view the photographic display of the pier's history. This is the last of the great pleasure piers, offering rides, romance, and perfect panoramic views of the bay and mountains.

Surfer on Santa Monica Beach.

The fulcrum of a 60-mile beachfront stretching from celebrity-riddled Malibu to the Palos Verdes Peninsula, Santa Monica is prime real estate, with stylish oceanfront hotels, an artsy atmosphere, and somewhat wacky residents. We never come here without spending at least some time hanging out at the **Third Street Promenade,** a pedestrian-only outdoor mall lined with shops and restaurants; we dig the **Fatburger,** an outpost of a legendary Southern California fast-food chain. Might as well go for the total SoCal experience.

ⓘ **Visitor Information Center,** 1920 Main St., Ste. B (ⓒ **800/544-5319** or 310/393-7593; www.santamonica.com).

✈ Los Angeles International.

🛏 $$ **Hotel Erwin,** 1697 Pacific Ave., Venice Beach (ⓒ **800/786-7789** or 310/452-1111; www.mphotel.com). $$$ **Oceana,** 849 Ocean Ave., Santa Monica (ⓒ **800/777-0758** or 310/393-0486; www.hoteloceanasantamonica.com).

WHY THEY'LL THANK YOU: Classic beach vibe.

Baseball Hall of Fame
Shrine to the Great American Pastime

Ages 6 & up • Cooperstown, New York

ADMITTEDLY MY FAMILY IS CRAZY FOR BASEBALL, BUT EVEN WHEN I LOOK at it objectively, I'd have to say that the **National Baseball Hall of Fame and Museum** in Cooperstown sets the gold standard for sports museums. The very word *Cooperstown* has become synonymous with baseball history, for legend (now discredited) claims that Abner Doubleday invented baseball here. Opened in 1939, the Hall of Fame has been around long enough to amass an unparalleled collection of sports memorabilia. You don't have to be a statistic-spouting baseball fanatic to feel moved by this homage to America's pastime.

The Hall's redbrick Federal-style facade looks as all-American as the game it represents. Laid out like a giant timeline, the Hall walks you through the **history of baseball,** starting with the various European ball-and-bat games that were its predecessors. Recent renovations have added more hands-on and interactive exhibits for kids, including a 13-minute multimedia show and a special area for toddlers and preschoolers, but it's the **memorabilia** that really tells the story, from Ty Cobb's glove to Babe Ruth's bat. You'll see the ridiculous scanty protective gear catchers used to wear behind the plate, the

Ty Cobb's plaque at the Baseball Hall of Fame.

gradual evolution of the regulation ball and bat, a panoply of uniforms through the decades, the ever-changing look of trading cards. You'll learn about the Black Sox scandal of 1919 and how baseball survived World War II. Special galleries are devoted to topics such as the Negro Leagues and the women's professional leagues. Snippets of vintage broadcasts and video footage of historic games are played at the touch of a button. Sure, my kids gravitated at first to exhibits paying tribute to today's stars and teams, set in a replica major-league locker room, but the more they saw of baseball's storied past—the actual objects, worn and discolored from play—the more they got into it. We saved a stroll through the actual Hall of Fame gallery for last, and by that time, those names on the plaques really meant something.

(i) 25 Main St. ((C) **888/HALL-OF-FAME** [425-5633] or 607/547-7200; www.baseballhalloffame.org).

✈ Albany International, 75 miles.

🛏 $ **Best Western Plus at the Commons,** 50 Commons Dr. ((C) **607/547-7100;** www.bwcooperstown.com). $$$ **Inn at Cooperstown,** 16 Chestnut St. ((C) **607/547-5756;** www.innatcooperstown.com).

WHY THEY'LL THANK YOU: Baseball is more than a game, it's a window on America.

90 For Sports Fans

Fenway Park
Where the Red Sox Rule

Ages 6 & up • Boston, Massachusetts

WHEN THE **BOSTON RED SOX** WON THE 2004 WORLD SERIES—ending an 86-year dry spell—and repeated the feat in 2007, they may have lost their status as one of baseball's most beloved underdogs, but I haven't heard any members of Red Sox Nation complaining. Sure, the Yankees, their perennial American League East rivals

A night game at Fenway Park.

down in New York City, have a higher payroll and more world titles. None of that matters to dedicated Red Sox supporters, and their numbers are legion. The 2005 movie *Fever Pitch* didn't exaggerate anything: Sit among them in the stands and you'll definitely remember that the word "fan" comes from "fanatic." But I, for one, never mind. You're watching ball in an intensely green place that's older than your grandparents, inhaling a Fenway Frank and wishing for a home run—what could be better?

My father was a Red Sox true believer his whole life, and though my family has committed the ultimate treason of rooting for the Yankees, we still harbor a secret fondness for the Sox. So it is that from time to time, we take off our Yankees caps and visit Fenway Park.

It's a venerable stadium, though "stadium" seems almost too grand a term for this, the oldest park in the major leagues (built in 1912). Its quirks only add to the Fenway mystique: the narrow seats, the hand-operated scoreboard, the 37-foot-high left-field wall known as the **"Green Monster"** for its tendency to rob opposing hitters of their home runs. Those seats may be uncomfortable but they're gratifyingly close to the field, without the wide swaths of grass other parks have put between the fans and the players.

Compared with its modern brethren, however, Fenway is tiny, and **tickets** are both expensive and hard to get. Throughout the season, a limited number of standing-room tickets go on sale the day of the game, and fans sometimes return presold tickets (especially if a rainout causes rescheduling). It can't hurt to check. Forced to choose between seats in a low-numbered grandstand section—say, 10 or below—and those in the bleachers, go for the bleachers. They can get rowdy during night games, but the view is better from there than from the deep right-field corner.

We took a **Fenway Park tour** (conducted year-round) that actually allowed us to peer inside the cramped space behind the Green Monster and walk out onto the warning track, stop in the press box, and visit the Red Sox Hall of Fame. Best of all was the guide's commentary, rich in team lore and highly entertaining.

ⓘ 4 Yawkey Way (✆ **877/REDSOX-9** [733-7699] for tickets, 617/226-6666 for tours; www.redsox.com).

✈ Boston Logan International.

🛏 $$ **DoubleTree Suites by Hilton,** 400 Soldiers Field Rd. (✆ **800/222-TREE** [8733] or 617/783-0090; www.doubletree.com). $ **The Midtown Hotel,** 220 Huntington Ave. (✆ **800/343-1177** or 617/262-1000; www.midtownhotel.com).

BEST TIME: Season runs March to October.

WHY THEY'LL THANK YOU: Baseball legends still matter here.

91   **For Sports Fans**

Wrigley Field
The Cubs' Den
Ages 4 & up • Chicago, Illinois

THE **CHICAGO CUBS** HAVEN'T PLAYED IN THE WORLD SERIES SINCE 1945 and haven't won the darn thing since 1908. When the Red Sox finally won a Series in 2004, the Cubs became undisputed holders of

Wrigley Field.

the crown for Most Beloved Losers. Chicagoans do love their Cubbies, champs or not, and there's no question that the team plays in one of baseball's classic venues, tiny Wrigley Field. Back in 1988, lights were finally installed for night play, but they're rarely used—the Cubs still play mostly day games. With its ivy-covered outfield walls, a hand-operated scoreboard, a view of Lake Michigan from the upper deck, and the El rattling past, it's old-fashioned baseball all the way, and our kids enjoyed every minute of their game there.

Built in 1914, Wrigley Field is the second-oldest venue in baseball (after Fenway Park), although the Cubs didn't move in until 1916 (a decade after their last Series victory!). Originally Weeghman Field, it was renamed in 1926 after the team's new owner, William Wrigley, Jr., the chewing-gum magnate.

No matter how the Cubs are doing in the standings, tickets go fast—most weekend and night games are sold out by Memorial Day. Your best bet is to hit a weekday game, where you'll be sitting alongside plenty of Chicagoans who called in sick to work and miraculously recovered by game time. Wrigley is small enough that every seat is a decent seat, and the place truly earns its nickname "The Friendly Confines"—every time I've been there, the fans around me were passionate, friendly, well-informed, and good-natured in the face of defeat. Riding the Red Line El to the Addison Street stop is part of the experience: You can look down into the park from the train, and hear the roar of the crowd as soon as you step onto the platform. During the regular season, you can take a 90-minute **tour** of the vintage stadium, visiting the press box, dugouts, both visitors' and Cubs' clubhouses, and the playing field itself; these tours are popular, so book in advance (☎ **773/404-CUBS**).

Just some of the **traditions** we love at Wrigley: Enterprising owners of surrounding houses have built stands on their roofs where they seat their own ticket holders; ground rules declare that if a ball gets stuck in the ivy, it's a double; and a pennant is flown after every game with a big "w" or "l" to alert passersby to the outcome of the game (who needs the Internet?). When the opposing team hits a home run out of the park, somebody on the sidewalk outside picks up the offending ball and throws it back over the wall. You've gotta love a ballpark where that happens.

ⓘ W. Addison St. (☎ **773/404-CUBS** [2827]; www.cubs.mlb.com).

✈ O'Hare International, 10 miles. Midway International, 12 miles.

🛏 $$ **Homewood Suites by Hilton,** 40 E. Grand Ave. (☎ **800/ CALL-HOME** [225-5466] or 312/644-2222; www.homewoodsuites chicago.com). $$ **Hotel Allegro Chicago,** 171 W. Randolph St. (☎ **800/643-1500** or 312/236-0123; www.allegrochicago.com).

WHY THEY'LL THANK YOU: Watching a Cubs homer sail over those ivy walls.

92 | **For Sports Fans**

Notre Dame
The Holy Land of College Football
Ages 8 & up (Notre Dame), 6 & up (Hall of Fame) •
South Bend, Indiana

FROM NOTRE DAME STADIUM, YOU CAN SEE A 132-FOOT-HIGH mosaic of Jesus on the side wall of the campus library—a mosaic shrewdly placed so that Christ, with upraised hands, is centered right over the north goal post. **Touchdown Jesus** is a fitting sight for this Catholic university in northern Indiana, which has had no fewer than eight national championships, seven Heisman Trophy winners, five number-one pro draft picks, and 96 All-Americans. You don't have to be an alum to be a rabid fan of Notre Dame football—you just have to love football, like my teenage son does.

Notre Dame has had a football team since 1887 (though its famous marching band is even older, the oldest in the country, formed in 1845). The redbrick stadium is vintage, built in 1930, the last year of famed coach Knute Rockne's decade at the school. Rockne, more than anyone, is responsible for the nationwide Notre Dame fan base, for he actively sought far-flung matches and developed cross-country rivalries, with such schools as Michigan, USC, Navy, and Boston College. Notre Dame's popularity nowadays transcends regional loyalties; they're the nation's only football team, pro or collegiate, whose entire schedule is broadcast on radio coast to coast, and since 1966 there's only been one home game that wasn't sold out. But here's the catch: All 80,000 seats to home games are allocated to season ticket holders, alumni, students, faculty, and parents of current students, although somehow they do pop up on ticket services (at inflated prices, of course). Call the ticket office at ✆ **574/631-7356** to inquire about last-minute tickets, or work your connections—find a Notre Dame alum or parent who'll buy tickets for you. Otherwise, you'll have to be content with buying merchandise at the Irish Shop in Eck Center, or taking a 1¼-hour, free, student-led **walking tour** of the beautiful rolling campus (✆ **574/631-5726**), which doesn't go inside the stadium.

There is, however, another reason to come to South Bend. In 1995, the **College Football Hall of Fame** moved from Kings Mills, Ohio, to a state-of-the-art facility in downtown South Bend. Built to look like a football stadium, with a green gridiron-lined outdoor plaza, the museum has, besides the honoree exhibits, plenty of interactive kiosks, a 360-degree theater where you can stand surrounded by the noisy blur of game-day action, and sizable interactive areas for testing your skills against some of the greatest players in college football history. Come soon, though—the Hall is slated to move to Atlanta in late 2013.

ⓘ **Notre Dame Stadium,** University of Notre Dame (✆ **574/631-7356;** www.und.collegesports.com). **College Football Hall of Fame,** 111 S. St. Joseph St. (✆ **800/440-FAME** [3263] or 574/235-9999; www.collegefootball.org).

✈ South Bend Regional.

🛏 $$ **Comfort Suites University Area,** 52939 S.R. 933 (✆ **877/424-6423** or 574/272-1500; www.choicehotels.com). $$ **Inn at St. Mary's,** 53993 S.R. 933 (✆ **800/947-8627** or 574/232-4000; www.innatsaintmarys.com).

WHY THEY'LL THANK YOU: Seeing Touchdown Jesus.

---

93 For Sports Fans

The Kentucky Derby
Bluegrass & Red Roses
Ages 4 & up • Louisville, Kentucky

As a kid, I must admit being disappointed that the grass wasn't bright blue in Kentucky bluegrass country, although it does have a bluish cast. Legend has it that this species of grass is the best for raising Thoroughbred racehorses. It must have some effect, because more than two-thirds of the winners of the Kentucky Derby—America's premier horse race—have been bred right here on Kentucky's splendid horse farms.

Louisville's **Churchill Downs** racetrack, its huge white-frame grandstand topped by a distinctive pair of slim gray spires, opened in 1875, and the Kentucky Derby—originally patterned after England's Epsom Derby—has been run every May since then. It's the first in the Triple Crown, a trio of renowned flat races for 3-year-olds, and its traditions have become famous, from the prerace singing of "My Old Kentucky Home" down to the garland of 554 red roses draped over the winning colt's neck. Grandstand seats for the Derby must be booked months ahead and cost a fortune; a more casual option is to join the euphoric crowd picnicking in the 40-acre infield (you won't see much of the race, but you'll experience a good party). The **Kentucky Derby Museum,** open year-round just outside Gate #1 (☎ **502/637-7097;** www.derbymuseum.org), has videos and hands-on exhibits (don't miss the one where you sit on a saddle in a real starting gate).

Before you hit the track, though, I suggest driving around the countryside near Lexington, 100 miles southeast of Louisville, to see where generations of Thoroughbred champions have been bred. The most famous horse farm, **Calumet Farm,** doesn't allow visitors, though you can do a drive-by with **Horse Farm Tours** (☎ **800/976-1034** or 859/268-2906; www.horsefarmtours.com), which then visits other working horse farms. You can tour **Claiborne Farm,** Winchester Road, Paris (☎ **859/233-4252;** www.claibornefarm.com), where Seabiscuit was born and Secretariat was a longtime stud stallion (his grave is on the farm), or **Three Chimneys Farm,** Old Frankfort Pike, Versailles (☎ **859/873-7053;** www.threechimneys.com), where Seattle Slew was the resident stud. The **Kentucky Horse Park,** 4089 Iron Works Pike, Lexington (☎ **800/678-8813** or 859/233-4303; www.kyhorsepark.com), has Man o' War's grave and a museum on horse history, but the real fun for kids is walking through the barns, seeing shows in the equestrian arena (April to Oct), and taking horse and pony rides.

ⓘ **Churchill Downs,** 700 Central Ave. (☎ **502/636-4400;** www.churchilldowns.com).

✈ Louisville International.

🛏 $$$ **Seelbach Hilton,** 500 Fourth St., Louisville (☎ **800/333-3399** or 502/585-3200; www.seelbachhilton.com). $$ **DoubleTree Suites by Hilton,** 2601 Richmond Rd., Lexington (☎ **800/222-TREE** [8733] or 859/268-0060; www.doubletree.com).

WHY THEY'LL THANK YOU: And they're off!

The Daytona 500
NASCAR Classic
Ages 4 & up • Daytona, Florida

LIKE MUCH ELSE IN FLORIDA, IT ALL BEGAN WITH A BEACH: BEAUTIFUL Daytona Beach, which runs for 24 miles along a skinny peninsula divided from the north Florida mainland by the Halifax River. In the early 1900s, when "horseless carriages" were still a novelty, automobile enthusiasts discovered that Daytona Beach's uniquely hard-packed white sand made the perfect drag strip. A century later, the town has every right to call itself "The World Center of Racing."

Auto racing in Daytona outgrew the beach long ago. In 1959, a proper 2½-mile racetrack, the **Daytona International Speedway,** was built 4 miles inland, and stock car racing's premier event, the 200-lap Daytona 500, was launched. The National Association for Stock Car Auto Racing (NASCAR) is now based in Daytona, and over a million race fans come here for 9 or 10 major events a year. Big races sell out months in advance—tickets to the Daytona 500 in February can be gone a year ahead of time (call ✆ **800/PITSHOP** [748-7467] for tickets).

If you're not attending a race, you can also take a 30-minute **guided tram tour** that visits the garage area, pit road, and so on. Speed freaks can pay a stiff fee to have the **Richard Petty Driving Experience,** run by seven-time Daytona 500 winner Richard Petty (✆ **800/237-3889;** www.drivepetty.com)—a three-lap ride around the tri-oval track in a real stock car, cruising at an average speed of, oh, say 115 mph.

ⓘ 1801 W. International Speedway Blvd. (✆ **800/PITSHOP** [748-7467]; www.daytonainternationalspeedway.com).

✈ Daytona Beach International.

🛏 $$ **Bahama House,** 2001 S. Atlantic Ave., Daytona Beach Shores (📞 **888/687-1894** or 386/248-2001; www.daytonabahama house.com). $$ **Shoreline All Suites Inn,** 2435 S. Atlantic Ave., Daytona Beach Shores (📞 **800/293-0653** or 386/252-1692; www. daytonashoreline.com).

WHY THEY'LL THANK YOU: Banking the turn into the home stretch.

Adrenaline Rushes **95**

Up in the Air in Sedona
Ballooning over the Great Red Rocks
Ages 8 & up • Sedona, Arizona

HOT-AIR BALLOONING IS EXTREMELY POPULAR IN THE SOUTHWEST— Albuquerque's annual balloon festival every October is the country's largest—and there are plenty of operators vying for your business. Beautiful as all these desert landscapes are, the one that's most thrilling to soar over, to my mind, is the red-rock country around Sedona, Arizona, with its wind-sculpted buttes and outcroppings thrusting up from the desert scrub, the rock glowing as if on fire.

These excursions are always early-morning affairs—you need still morning air to properly inflate the balloon and to ensure a stable takeoff. The entire outing may take as much as 3 hours, of which only an hour or so is actually in the air. But the kids will enjoy watching the limp silk billow into shape as burners inflate the balloon and, once you've settled back to earth, having a breakfast picnic in the desert while waiting for the "chase team" to arrive, deflate the balloon, and pack it back into its sack. Gondolas suspended below the balloons carry up to seven passengers at a time, and the ride is surprisingly steady—instead of fighting wind currents, you're going with the flow. True, the pace is often slow and majestic rather than

The red rocks of Sedona.

death defying. Still, you're high up and protected only by the wicker sides of the basket, which is thrilling enough.

Both **Northern Light Balloon Expeditions** (✆ **800/230-6222** or 928/282-2274; www.northernlightballoon.com) and **Red Rock Balloon Adventures** (✆ **800/258-3754** or 928/284-0040; www. redrockballoons.com) are licensed to fly over the spectacular Coconino National Forest. In flight, their pilots will chat with the kids about the landscape they're flying over and about the science and art of hot-air ballooning.

ⓘ **Sedona Visitor Center,** 331 Forest Rd. (✆ **800/288-7336** or 928/282-7722; www.visitsedona.com).

✈ Phoenix Sky Harbor International, 116 miles.

🛏 $$ **Best Western Plus Inn of Sedona,** 1200 W. Hwy. 89A (✆ **800/292-6344** or 928/282-3072; www.innofsedona.com). $$$ **Hilton Sedona Resort,** 90 Ridge Trail Dr. (✆ **877/2REDROCK** [273-3762] or 928/284-4040; www.hiltonsedona.com).

WHY THEY'LL THANK YOU: Up, up, and away.

The Call of the Wild in Denali
Your Own Personal Iditarod
Ages 10 & up • Denali National Park, Alaska

ALASKA'S DENALI NATIONAL PARK IS A PRISTINE WILDERNESS, AND IN an attempt to keep it that way, the Parks Service permits no public access by automobile—there's only one gravel road through the center of the park, which you can travel on a shuttle bus that links rest stops and campgrounds and lodges and scenic overlooks. Disembarking at various points, parkgoers can then hike into the tundra as far as they wish, though most folks seem content just to ride the bus and look out the window at those incredible Arctic views. But there's another way to get even deeper into this stunning wilderness—by racing over the snowy backcountry on a **dog sled,** just as the park rangers do.

Two outfits have been approved to run wintertime dog-sledding packages into Denali, using their own rustic lodges as home base (guests sleep in private log cabins near the lodges). Both of these lodges are just outside the park, but so close that they feature views of majestic Mount McKinley, America's biggest mountain. **Denali West Lodge,** set on the shore of Lake Minchumina, is the smaller of the two operations (only eight guests at a time), and so remote that you'll need to fly in on a little private plane. It offers everything from day trips from the lodge to 9-day mushing expeditions. You can drive via Alaska Hwy. 3 to **EarthSong Lodge,** which runs day trips and 3- to 10-day dog-sledding camp-outs (using tents or outlying cabins), although itineraries can be tailored to guests' interests. Each guest 12 and over drives his or her own sled, with teams of four to six huskies. (Younger children may simply ride along on the sled.) EarthSong even offers an option for summer visitors to get a taste of the dog-sledding experience by driving a husky team with a wheeled cart.

It may sound as if you'd need special skills, but the proprietors of both lodges are longtime mushers experienced in training

Denali National Park.

first-timers. You just need to be strong enough to hold on tight as the dogs surge forward, whipping you over the snowy track. Perhaps 4 or 5 hours of the day is spent mushing, covering on average 30 miles of terrain, across the snowy tundra, around lakes, through taiga forests and glacial river valleys. You're practically guaranteed sightings of moose, caribou, Dall sheep, foxes, lynx, wolverines, and beavers; your chances of running across other human beings, however, are practically nil. Nighttime camp-outs may be lit by the Northern Lights and serenaded by nearby wolves, howling in sync with the huskies. Now *that's* getting away from it all.

(i) Denali Park Rd. ((©) **907/683-2294;** www.nps.gov/dena).

✈ Fairbanks International, 125 miles. Ted Stevens Anchorage International, 236 miles.

🚂 **Alaska Railroad** ((©) **800/544-0552** or 907/265-2494; www.alaskarailroad.com) runs trains from Anchorage (7½ hr.) and from Fairbanks (4 hr.), summers only.

🛏 $$$ **Denali West Lodge** (📞 **907/674-3112;** www.denali westlodge.com). $$$ **EarthSong Lodge** (📞 **907/683-2863;** www. earthsonglodge.com).

BEST TIME: November to March.

WHY THEY'LL THANK YOU: Bonding with the huskies.

Roller Coasters

97

The Cyclone
The Coaster That Made Coney Island Famous

Ages 8 & up • Brooklyn, New York

Back in the days before air-conditioning, New York families flocked to the beach at Coney Island to cool off in summer, and it was a rite of passage to grow tall enough (54 in.) to be allowed on New York's most famous roller coaster, the **Cyclone.** Thrill rides may have advanced technologically since then, but this classic coaster, built in 1927, is still one of the best, plunging a heart-stopping eight stories from its highest peak.

The charms of Coney Island go well beyond the Cyclone, of course; for one thing, there's that dynamite location, right on a wide white-sand beach where Atlantic waters crash. The **New York Aquarium,** Surf Avenue and West 8th Street (📞 **718/265-FISH** [3474]; www.nyaquarium.com), just a short stroll up the boardwalk, features dolphins, sea lions, seals, and walruses. At 12th Street, Deno's Wonder Wheel Amusement Park (www.wonderwheel.com) features the 1920 landmark **Wonder Wheel,** an ingenious double Ferris wheel of gargantuan proportions. For those who like to stay closer to earth, there are bumper cars, tilt-a-whirls, spinning tea-cups, carousels, and kiddie rides, as well as satisfyingly cheesy arcades; the area also has mini-golf and go-kart concessions. Compared to huge plasticized theme parks such as Disney, Six Flags, and Busch Gardens, the Coney Island amusements have a grungy

Coney Island's Wonder Wheel.

midway glamour that older kids will appreciate—it's the Real Thing. (With kids, it's best to visit by day—and know where your wallet is at all times.)

The beach and boardwalk have been spruced up lately, though, and the beachfront souvenir shops and food stands have acquired a post-modern hipster gloss, with Brooklyn artists decorating their side walls with retro murals. Even the local freak show, tucked up a Surf Avenue side street near the parks, has the whiff of a performance art installation, and along the boardwalk to the east, there's a tidy baseball stadium for a popular Mets farm team, the **Brooklyn Cyclones** (© **718/449-8497;** www.brooklyncyclones.com). But you can still get a reliable kosher frank at Nathan's famous open-air hot dog stand on Surf Avenue—some things never change.

ⓘ Surf Avenue (www.coneyislandfunguide.com).

✈ John F. Kennedy International, LaGuardia, Newark Liberty International.

🛏 $$ **Excelsior Hotel,** 45 W. 81st St. (📞 **800/368-4575** or 212/
362-9200; www.excelsiorhotelny.com). $$$ **Le Parker Meridien,**
119 W. 56th St. (pedestrian entrance: 118 W. 57th St.; 📞 **800/543-
4300** or 212/245-5000; www.parkermeridien.com).

BEST TIME: Amusement parks open daily June to Labor Day, Saturday and Sunday April to May and September to October.

WHY THEY'LL THANK YOU: Atmosphere, atmosphere, atmosphere.

Roller Coasters

98

Millennium Force
Cedar Point's Record Setter
Ages 10 & up • Sandusky, Ohio

WHEN IT OPENED IN 2000, THE MILLENNIUM FORCE AT OHIO'S
Cedar Point amusement park not only was the world's tallest
roller coaster (310 ft.), but also had the longest drop (300 ft.), the
steepest banked turns of any noninverted coaster (122 degrees), and
the fastest speed (93 mph). It may climb up that 310-foot peak
(taller than the Statue of Liberty) at a modest 45-degree angle, but
it plunges down the other side angled at 80 degrees. It covers
more than a mile in length, speeding to its finish line in 2 minutes
and 20 seconds, almost before you know what hit you. But no
record is unbreakable. Within 3 years, the Millennium Force was
surpassed—by another roller coaster at Cedar Point, of course.

There's no question that Cedar Point prides itself on its roller
coasters—it has 17 of them, among the newest being the **Top Thrill
Dragster,** which debuted in 2003. Top Thrill accelerates like a dragster right out of the gate, taking only 4 seconds to reach 120 mph,
and then climbs *straight up,* perpendicular to the ground, to a height
of 420 feet, the equivalent of a 42-story building. And what does it do
next? It drops down just as steeply (again at 120 mph), throwing in a
wrenching 270-degree twist. The **Wicked Twister** is another heart-
in-your-mouth experience, a U-shaped suspended coaster that

ping-pongs back and forth between two 215-foot-high towers, corkscrewing up and down each tower, three times forward and twice backward, reaching a speed of up to 70 mph. Each of these coasters has its rabid fans, while others are passionate about the experience on **Magnum,** or **Raptor,** or **Gemini,** or **Blue Streak,** or any of the other innovative steel coasters at Cedar Point.

Cedar Point has 75 rides in all and that's not even counting the attractions at the adjoining 18-acre outdoor water park, **Soak City** (open Memorial Day to Labor Day). An indoor water park, **Castaway Bay,** recently opened to extend the season. Five resort hotels and an RV park on the 364-acre property are available for those who need more than 1 day to do all the rides.

ⓘ 1 Cedar Point Dr. (✆ **419/627-2350;** www.cedarpoint.com).

✈ Cleveland Hopkins International, 54 miles.

🛏 $$ **Cleveland Marriott Downtown at Key Center,** 127 Public Sq., Cleveland (✆ **888/236-2427** or 216/696-9200; www.marriott.com). $$ **DoubleTree by Hilton Cleveland Downtown/Lakeside,** 1111 Lakeside Ave., Cleveland (✆ **800/222-TREE** [8733] or 216/241-5100; www.doubletree.com).

BEST TIME: Open daily mid-May through early September; weekends in September and October.

WHY THEY'LL THANK YOU: That moment at the peak, before the drop. Multiplied 16 times.

The Santa Cruz Boardwalk
California Classic by the Sea
All ages • Santa Cruz, California

ONE OF THE FEW OLD-FASHIONED AMUSEMENT PARKS LEFT IN THE world, the Santa Cruz Beach Boardwalk is California's answer to

Rye Playland. Situated next to Santa Cruz's lovely mile-long public beach, the boardwalk is a half-mile strip of rides, shops, and restaurants, harking back to an era of seaside innocent fun. It's the sort of classic site you don't necessarily expect on the West Coast.

The park has 35 rides, two of them historic landmarks. The **Looff Carousel,** built in 1911 by Charles I. D. Looff, boasts hand-carved wooden horses, a 342-pipe organ band, and one of the few brass ring grabs left in existence; snatch the brass ring as your horse whirls past the post, and then throw it into a painted clown's mouth to win a free ride. Looff's son, Arthur Looff, designed the park's other landmark, the red-and-white 1924 **Giant Dipper** roller coaster, which offers great views of Monterey Bay from its peaks—though few riders manage to take them in while being hurtled up and down at 55 mph. They have a split second longer to enjoy the views from the top of the 125-foot-tall **Double Shot** drop tower. A host of other thrill rides trade on speed, with such names as **Hurricane, Tornado,** and **Tsunami;** indoor "dark rides" include the **Haunted Castle** and **Ghost Blasters,** though I prefer the 1961-vintage **Cave Train,** where glow-in-the-dark prehistoric characters pop out. There is a section of smaller-scale rides for the under-36-inch crowd as well.

Although there's no admission fee to get onto the boardwalk, the individual ride tickets can mount up fast—an "unlimited rides" bracelet, which at first doesn't seem cheap, could end up saving you money. The beach boardwalk keeps seasonal hours, open daily from April through Labor Day but only on weekends and holidays throughout the winter and fall.

ⓘ 400 Beach St. (✆ **831/426-7433;** www.beachboardwalk.com).

✈ San Jose International, 33 miles. San Francisco International, 77 miles.

🛏 $$ **Fern River Resort,** 5250 Hwy. 9, Felton (✆ **831/335-4412;** www.fernriver.com).

WHY THEY'LL THANK YOU: Screaming from the top of the Giant Dipper.

The Mall of America
Minnesota's Mega-Mall Amusements
All ages • Bloomington, Minnesota

WHAT NERVE IT TOOK TO BUILD A SHOPPING CENTER IN SUBURBAN Minnesota and call it the Mall of America. And yet there is something iconic about this over-the-top shrine to consumerism. Subscribing to the all-American bigger-is-better philosophy, the mall could hold seven Yankee Stadiums or 258 Statues of Liberty; walk one circuit around a level of stores and you've clocked nearly a mile. There are over 520 stores at this huge retail center 20 minutes south of downtown Minneapolis, stacked on four brightly lit levels around a central glass atrium—not only that, but 14 movie screens, a food court, 20 sit-down restaurants, half a dozen attractions, and even a wedding chapel. You've got to see it to believe it.

The main attraction is **Nickelodeon Universe,** America's largest enclosed theme park, which covers 7 ground-floor acres in the immense central atrium with more than 27 rides, including a kiddie roller coaster that loops around large planters full of trees. This will thrill toddlers and young grade schoolers; kids who've outgrown those tame rides will still enjoy the **Sea Life Minnesota Aquarium,** where 10,000 sea creatures swim around in tanks on a subterranean level. Between the virtual submarine ride and the "shark encounter"— a glass tunnel that walks you through a shark tank—it's like a mini–Sea World. At the mall. For teens or preteens (and, admit it, adults too), the **A.C.E.S Flight Simulator** lets you play virtual pilot on an F-18 Hornet jet or a WWII-era P-51 Mustang.

While not strictly a theme attraction (no admission charge, for one thing), the four-story **Lego store** is as good as a ride, with some 90 life-size Lego models to marvel at; the **Build-a-Bear Workshop** is another store that offers plenty of entertainment. So what if most of the other shops are the usual gang of chain stores? It's called the Mall of America, dude—so who's expecting snooty high-end retail? It's supersize, it's commercial, and it caters to the masses—and there's nothing more American than that. ·

(i) 60 E. Broadway ((C) **952/883-8800;** www.mallofamerica.com).

✈ Minneapolis–St. Paul International.

🛏 $ **Best Western Plus Kelly Inn,** 161 St. Anthony Ave., St. Paul ((C) **800/780-7234** or 651/227-8711; www.bestwesternstpaul.com).

WHY THEY'LL THANK YOU: Flying planes and walking through a shark tank.

Indexes

General Index

Geographical Index

Photo Credits

Photo Credits